FLORA POETICA

The Chatto Book of Botanical Verse

Edited, with an introduction, by
Sarah Maguire

Chatto & Windus
LONDON

Published by Chatto & Windus 2003

2 4 6 8 10 9 7 5 3 1

First published in Great Britain in 2001 by
Chatto & Windus
Random House, 20 Vauxhall Bridge Road,
London SW1V 2SA

Random House Australia (Pty) Limited
20 Alfred Street, Milsons Point, Sydney,
New South Wales 2061, Australia

Random House New Zealand Limited
18 Poland Road, Glenfield,
Auckland 10, New Zealand

Random House South Africa (Pty) Limited
Endulini, 5A Jubilee Road, Parktown, 2193, South Africa

The Random House Group Limited Reg. No. 954009
www.randomhouse.co.uk

A CIP catalogue record for this book
is available from the British Library

ISBN 0 7011 6923 0

Papers used by Random House are natural,
recyclable products made from wood grown in sustainable forests;
the manufacturing processes conform to the environmental
regulations of the country of origin

Printed and bound in Great Britain by
Biddles Ltd, Guildford and Kings Lynn

a roses for seitlhamo

Contents

Introduction

If I hadn't been eased out of formal education at the age of seventeen, you would never have held this book in your hands. Straight after being ejected from school, I began working as an apprentice gardener for the London Borough of Ealing, and I stayed on for the next three years until I'd obtained my City & Guilds' Horticulture qualifications. Most of the time it was tough, repetitive manual labour: raking-up leaves every single day for seven weeks at a stretch; double-digging trenches in the poisoned London clay; lifting turf, laying turf; emptying litter bins full of rotten food and pornography; weeding and hoeing and weeding; sweeping the paths and, on the days when it snowed on the paths, rearranging the snow round the park. Walpole Park in Ealing Broadway. You can still sit out under some of the trees I planted decades ago.

Since leaving the Parks Department I've hardly ever picked up a hoe. But I did keep the language. Twice a week for three years I had to take part in a 'plant ident': a small exam where we were expected to come up with the botanical names — genus, species and variety — for a random selection of seeds, solitary blooms, noxious weeds and odd bits of twig. I have a very clear memory of travelling home from work absolutely exhausted one evening during those early weeks of gardening, and suddenly realising I now lived in a completely different world. A big ugly shrub I'd passed every day on the bus since I was small, caught my attention for the very first time. 'That's an *Aucuba japonica* "Crotonoides"', I remembered. And it was. But it wasn't just necessity that made me learn the names of plants. It was pleasure. I loved the sound of these strange words, their Latinate abstractions, the sense of order they implied. One of the things that kept me sane during freezing hours of mind-numbing tasks was reciting a litany of all the plants within sight. And I'm still delighted and astonished when, even now, the botanical identity of some nondescript shrub swims into view. The names of grass seeds have stayed with me (I looked after a bowling green during the drought of '76), as have fungal infections, mineral deficiencies, botanical terminology and the proprietory names of organophosphate chemicals, now absolutely illegal throughout the western world.

When I started writing poetry in my mid-twenties, I discovered that this language was working its way into my poems, even more insistently as the years went by. There are gardens mentioned in my first book, *Spilt Milk*, but by my second, *The Invisible Mender*, a whole section of the book was taken over by my experiences as an apprentice gardener. More recently, I've found myself writing poems about individual flowers, using the plants as a starting point for poems that take off in many different directions, such as the night-time bike-ride through the suburbs of Marrakesh in my poem called 'Hibiscus'[1]. As a result of this growing obsession, I have become increasingly alert to how other poets turned to plants as subject matter, and I would often find myself thumbing through volumes of verse in bookshops and libraries, lighting on the names of plants among the stanzas.

In 1998 I became the Poet in Residence at Chelsea Physic Garden[2]. I soon realised that, in order to best explore the connections between botany and poetry, I needed to collect as many poems as I could about plants and gardens. Initially, this informal gathering was simply a teaching tool I used to help people find ways to approach writing about the garden. Then I began to create 'poetry labels' (which looked like plant labels but had lines of poetry engraved on them) to plant next to appropriate trees, shrubs and flowers. Eventually, after months in the British Library behaving like a bibliophile version of an obsessive eighteenth-century plant hunter, I realised I'd amassed an entire filing cabinet full of garden poems. At which point it seemed a good idea to share these discoveries with a wider public than the visitors to Chelsea Physic Garden.

When I began compiling this anthology, I had the vague notion that older English poetry would be particularly floral — encouraged perhaps by the abundance of flower references in Shakespeare. But whilst many of Shakespeare's contemporaries may name flowers in their verse, I discovered that very few of them take a specific tree or flower as the subject of a poem — the criterion for being included in *Flora Poetica*. In fact, such poems are relatively rare until the Romantic period, and it's not until the twentieth century that poets really begin to write about a large variety of plant species.

The first English poet to write poems about many individual flowers was Robert Herrick (1591–1674), and in *Flora Poetica* I've included his lyrics about daffodils, daisies, rosemary, tulips, primroses, violets and a willow tree. Herrick was writing just after the

Flemish painters, Jan Bruegel (1568–1625) and Ambrosius Bosschaert (1573–1621), had initiated the genre of flower painting in European art. This period also marked the arrival in Europe of an astonishing number of new plant species — notably tulips, narcissi, hyacinths, crown imperials, irises, anemones and lilies — largely from the Levant as a result of the first political contacts made with the Ottoman Empire in the mid-sixteenth century. During the next century, twenty times as many plants were to enter Europe as had arrived during the previous two thousand years[3]. As a result, plants no longer were cultivated primarily for medicinal purposes. For the first time in northern Europe botany began to develop as a science, ornamental gardening was widespread, and collecting decorative plants became an increasingly fashionable hobby — culminating in the 'Tulip Fever' which gripped the Netherlands in the 1630s[4].

As Joseph Addison noted in *The Spectator* in 1711, left entirely to its own natural devices, Britain would have been something of a horticultural backwater:

> If we consider our own Country in its Natural Prospect, without any of the Benefits and Advantages of Commerce, what a barren uncomfortable Spot of Earth falls to our Share! Natural Historians tell us, that no Fruit grows Originally among us, besides Hips and Haws, Acorns and Pig-Nutts, with other Delicates of the like Nature; That our Climate of itself, and without the Assistance of Art, can make no further Advances towards a Plumb than to a Sloe, and carries an Apple to no greater perfection than a Crab.[5]

At the time Addison was writing, Britain was witnessing an extraordinary explosion in the variety of plants available to gardeners and botanists. 'The Benefits and Advantages of Commerce', to which Addison refers, were Britain's burgeoning colonial interests. Without colonisation this breathtaking proliferation of different plant species would never have sprung up in British soil[6]. The growing prosperity of British society from the seventeenth century onwards gave more people the space, leisure and income to invest in gardens. And, as garden plants became a viable economic proposition, so plant hunters returned from distant places with exotics, eagerly bought by a fashion-conscious, horticulturally-minded British public[7]. This mass transplantation from distant lands is the subject of Kathleen Jamie's poem 'Rhododendrons', which describes how the shrubs travelled from the Himalayas to Scotland, to take root in 'our slightly acid soil'.

The fashion for exotic garden species, and the wealth which made their cultivation possible, was largely the result of the commercial trade in other kinds of plants: the aggressive expansion of the British Empire enabled vast fortunes to be made from cash-crops such as sugar, tea, tobacco, opium, quinine, coffee, cocoa, cotton and rubber, via the slave labour exploited to cultivate the crops[8]. In her poem 'Cinnamon Roots' the Sri Lankan poet Seni Seneviratne describes how the rare spices native to her homeland first lured European traders there, a move which later led to the establishment of plantations and to the island's colonisation. It's impossible to understand the significance of plants in British culture without grasping the centrality of colonialism. Addison's horticultural diagnosis is correct: were it not for 'Commerce', British gardens would be limited to little more than 'Hips and Haws'.

No poet in seventeenth-century Britain could possibly have written a poem about an exotic such as an amaryllis, as the contemporary poets Jorie Graham and James Lasdun do, because we know they'd never seen one: the spectacular 'belladonna lily' (*Amaryllis belladonna*) was first introduced to Britain in 1774 by Francis Masson, who brought it back from the Cape Province, now in the Republic of South Africa[9]. Before the Romantic period nearly all poets write about roses when they choose a specific plant as the sole subject of a poem. In fact, the two oldest poems in *Flora Poetica* (*c.* 1325–50) are concerned with Addison's 'Hips and Haws': one referring to a rose, 'Al Night by the Rosë, Rosë', and the other, 'Of Every Kinnë Tre', to a hawthorn. Other indigenous species crop up in John Donne's 'The Primrose' (1633) and Aphra Behn's 'On a Juniper-Tree' (1684). Mildmay Fane's 'Walk of Bay Trees' (1648) and George Wither's 'Marigold' (1634) were introduced to Britain by the Romans[10].

However, Herrick's 'To a Bed of Tulips' (1648) makes a direct reference to the growing horticultural diversity of his time, and in the wonderful garden poems written by Andrew Marvell (1621–78) a huge number of plants are mentioned, many of which had only recently arrived in Britain. Sadly, I've not been able to include any poems by Marvell in *Flora Poetica* since he never writes a whole poem about a specific plant. But this exclusion has led me to plot a companion anthology of poems devoted to gardens which would give Marvell the central place he rightly deserves in any collection of literature about plants and gardens.

Another famous poem on a horticultural theme that has failed to make it into *Flora Poetica* (that will also have to wait for my garden poems anthology) is George Herbert's 'The Flower' (1633) because the flower he's considering is botanically unidentifiable. Referring to a particular flower was irrelevant to Herbert, since any species would serve his poem's purpose of illuminating spiritual decline and reinvigoration. Similarly, Herrick wasn't writing about the individual flowers themselves, but using them as symbols. Despite their diverse floral titles, his lyrics mainly reiterate the common theme of *carpe diem*, as his best-known poem, 'To the Virgins, to Make Much of Time', makes clear:

> Gather ye Rosebuds while ye may,
> Old Time is still a-flying:
> And this same flower that smiles to-day
> To-morrow will be dying.

Likewise, John Donne (1572–1631) is more concerned with occult numerology in his poem 'The Primrose', not *Primula vulgaris* as such, and he employs the five-petalled primrose as a conceit to puzzle over whether women can be 'true' or not. This is hardly surprising if you consider that, when Donne and Herrick were writing, although plants were subjected to increasingly detailed inspection, the science of botany didn't yet exist[11]. Before the Enlightenment plants were part of an ordered and hierarchical world, the divinely-ordained Book of Nature. Although their close study was encouraged, as the work of artists such as Albrecht Dürer (1471–1528) and Leonardo da Vinci (1452–1519) demonstrates so clearly, this was intended to reveal their inner 'truth' rather than subject them to empirical scrutiny[12]. Pre-Enlightenment knowledge of plants was dominated by Neoplatonic ideas in which the signs on the surface of a plant, if correctly interpreted, could give precious information as to its true meaning and purpose — a theory commonly known as 'the doctrine of signatures'.

The exotic plants newly arrived in Britain from the colonies may have excited Marvell to include them in his poetic gardens, but they lacked the symbolic associations necessary for poets to take them as the subject of a poem. Plants, in poems, were interesting as symbols of something other than themselves. The small number of species represented in the poems here written before the late eighteenth century either already had symbolic value, such as the noble associations of Mildmay Fane's bay trees; are symbolically interchangeable, like Herrick's diverse blossoms; or are chosen for a detail which enables the poet to employ them as symbols, for example the five petals of Donne's primrose. Writing in detail about the botanical structure of plants, examining them as *objects*, was simply unimaginable to poets before the Romantic period, and only began to take place frequently during the twentieth century.

Of all flowers, the rose is unsurpassed in its rich symbolic associations. It was a symbol of the Virgin Mary from early Christian times and, as Greek and Roman classical literature became available again during the Renaissance, the reawakening of its earlier connection with Venus made it into the most potent floral symbol of desire, a status it still claims today. There are more poems in *Flora Poetica* about roses than any other plant, and they refer to a variety of subjects, though romantic desire remains by far the most popular. Divine love is the subject of two poems, written five centuries apart, which both address the Virgin Mary: 'Ther Is No Rose of Swych Virtú' (*c.* 1450) and Norman Nicolson's 'The Burning Rose' (1948). 'The Burning Rose' also happens to be the title of Frank Chipasula's very different poem written in 1990 about political violence in Malawi. And this poem, like the others near it, such as Seitlhamo Motsapi's explosively joyous, 'a roses for the folks we know', remind us that roses can signify revolutionary passion — the old leftist demand for 'bread and roses' — just as well as religious devotion, or desire and its disappointments.

Other old, often ancient, flower associations continue to be referred to by contemporary poets. In his poem about holly, 'Of Prickbush' (1989), Peter Redgrove remembers the Cornish traditions inspired by the plant; and Don Paterson in 'Twinflooer' (2001) recalls the Scottish legend which gave the flower its name. It seems that centuries of dispassionate botanical examination have not completely unsettled the arcane powers of plants[13]. Although nowadays we may be able to distinguish which plants can feed us, poison us, or drive us mad — and we no longer attribute their arrival to occult powers of spontaneous generation — plants still remain potent symbols of our mortal state, of the troubling frailty of our desires.

The first poet to really examine plants, and the rest of the natural world, with the patient care of a naturalist was John Clare (1793–1864). Clare was brought up in rural Northamptonshire, where he worked as a day labourer and hedge-setter, at a time when enclosure was forcing the rural population into desperate poverty and the English countryside was being transformed beyond recognition. Clare's astonishingly moving poems are full of beautifully-observed details which only someone who had spent long hours examining the wild flowers around him could have written. In turning lowly 'weeds' into English poetry, Clare's flower poems can be seen both as a political act — giving weight and dignity to 'common' plants — and as a gesture of love, a refusal to allow all that is being lost to pass by unrecorded.

Even though Clare was writing at a time when botany was becoming an increasingly popular pursuit — particularly amongst women, for whom plant collecting offered welcome opportunities for outdoor exercise as well as intellectual stimulation[14] — Clare's close attention to the details of plants is unusual amongst poets of the Romantic period. In poems such as Coleridge's 'This Lime-Tree Bower My Prison' (1834) and Wordsworth's 'I Wandered Lonely as a Cloud' (1807) — probably the most famous flower poem in the English language — the natural world is used as a metaphor to explore the poet's state of mind. William Blake, Anna Seward, Mary Tighe and Anna Laetitia Barbauld are also far more concerned with symbolism than naturalism when they look at flowers. One Romantic poet who knew a great deal about plants was John Keats, who studied medical botany at Guy's Hospital. But although he wrote poems full of informed references to plants, he never focussed his attention on a particular plant through the length of a poem and so I've had to exclude him from *Flora Poetica*[15]. Wordsworth's 'The Small Celandine' is therefore one of the rare examples of a Romantic poet demonstrating a botanical eye for detail. In May 1800 Dorothy Wordsworth wrote in her *Grasmere Journal*, 'Oh! that we had a book of botany'; later that year she and William acquired a copy of 'Withering's Botany', the most popular handbook then in print[16]. 'The Small Celandine' was published in 1807, so perhaps we can imagine that the botanising outings taken by the Wordsworths inspired William to write the poem from this close perspective.

This passion for all things botanical can be traced back to one man: the Swedish botanist Carl Linnaeus (1707–78). Linnaeus cleverly synthesised developments which had been taking place in the study of plants during the seventeenth and early eighteenth centuries, thus making botany both lucid and approachable — and therefore popular. His basic classification system continues to be used today.

Linnaeus grouped plants into genera and species, giving them two (Latin) names[17]. He then collected the genera into larger plant families. For example, the botanical name for the commonest rhododendron found in Britain, though not a native, and often considered an eyesore (see Ted Hughes' poem on the subject, 'Rhododendrons') is *Rhododendron ponticum*, *Rhododendron* being its genus and *ponticum* its species. Rhododendrons belong to the plant family Ericaceae, commonly known as the heather family[18]. At first sight it may seem strange that rhododendrons and heathers are related. However, a very close look at the structure of the flowers, especially if you remember some basic botany, will give you a clue: they both share the same number of male and female reproductive parts arranged in the same way, the key to Linnaeus' ordering principle.

As the flower poems I was collecting began to fill my filing cabinet, it became increasingly important to find a way to arrange them. Since the most rewarding aspect of researching this anthology was discovering poems, often written centuries apart, about the same plant, I realised that ordering them chronologically or alphabetically by title wouldn't work: both schemes would have scattered poems concerning the same plant — or closely related species such as heartsease, violets and pansies — throughout the book. It occurred to me that Linnaeus' classification system might be the best solution. If I identified the plant in each poem with its botanical name this would mean that whatever the date of the poem, or name the poet gave it, poems about the same plant could be collected together. Using Linnaeus' scheme meant the strange juxtapositions which I found so engaging could be maintained. One of my favourites is William Blake's 'Ah Sunflower' next to Allen Ginsberg's 'Sunflower Sutra', in which Ginsberg mentions Blake. The scheme has also permitted a delightful bunch of daffodil poems to flower together. No poet can write about daffodils without having Wordsworth in mind, and indeed, Michael Longley's moving lyric 'Daffodils' directly refers to 'I Wandered Lonely as a Cloud' and the significance it has for readers of English verse. I also felt pleased to place Ted Hughes' magnificent 'Daffodils' next to Sylvia Plath's 'Among the Narcissi' since both poems are provoked by the same events.

The popular interest in botany which provoked attention to Britain's indigenous and local flowers — like Wordsworth's daffodils and small Celandine — reached its peak during the late-eighteenth and early-nineteenth centuries. But it was cultivated flowers which were to become particularly fashionable during the Victorian era; for the rich, and the upwardly mobile, they were an important marker of status and wealth — much as they continue to be today. As increasing numbers of exotic plants were imported into Britain throughout the eighteenth century, improvements in technology (especially the thinner sheet-glass developed by Joseph Paxton at Chatsworth in the 1820s) permitted the construction of more glasshouses and conservatories. These hothouses were essential for growing delicate exotics, which were in great demand both for elaborate displays in Victorian country houses and for sale in the large number of florists' shops opening up in the cities. The 'language of flowers' — sending secret messages through the code of different blooms — was a Victorian obsession, and poetry about flowers was popular too. Much of it makes sickly reading nowadays, and I've tried to choose poems that have survived the profound shift of taste between that era and our own. Outstanding amongst them are a number of poems by women poets such as Emily Dickinson (1830–86) and Christina Rossetti (1830–94), both of whom use flowers as an oblique commentary on their desires and constraints.

Dickinson and Rossetti turned to flowers as metaphors of femininity because the cultural associations linking flowers and women were, and are, so deep-seated as to be almost unquestioned. The term 'deflowering' referred to the loss of a woman's virginity and 'flowers' was a wide-spread euphemism for menstruation during the nineteenth century. Naming a boy after a flower or decorating his room with floral wallpaper, giving a man a bouquet of flowers or a heady floral perfume, even now can only be done with an edge of irony or subversion, as a challenge to traditional male heterosexual identity. The unease the association between men and flowers can still provoke is made clear in Fred Voss' poem, 'A Threat' (1998). Voss records how the other men in the factory where he works fear him and call him crazy because 'They don't like the poetry I read'; the poet's unmasculine behaviour makes them look at him 'like they want to cut my balls off'. But he decides to hit back with something even more threatening than poetry:

> Tomorrow I think I will start bringing roses to work.
> Each day I will stand a rose in a jar of water
> on the workbench behind my machine.
> I want to really terrify my fellow workers
> this time.

It's interesting to remember in this context that gay men are often called 'pansies', and that many have adopted floral tropes for their own defiant purposes[19]. To this day, flowers continue to be a significant marker of gender identity and of sexual orientation.

The association between women and blossoms may seem rather pretty and harmless, but flowers, as many of the poets in this anthology repeatedly tell us, are decorative and silent and have no function once they've faded. Traditionally, men poets often turn to flowers to remind the women who resist them of their mortal vulnerability. Robert Herrick's floral *carpe diem* lyrics are an obvious example, as is Edmund Waller's famous poem, 'Go Lovely Rose' (1645). Conversely, other men poets compare women to flowers to express disgust at their sexual openness; Ted Hughes' poems 'Sketch of a Goddess', 'Sunstruck Foxglove' and 'Big Poppy' are powerful examples of the latter tendency, as are Howard Nemerov's 'Dandelions' and Ted Walker's 'Cuckoo Pint'.

At a time when the subjects considered suitable for women poets to tackle were very narrow indeed[20], they were allowed to write poems about traditionally feminine flowers whilst other topics were still considered inappropriately masculine. Given the range of powerful feelings stirred up by the relationship between women and flowers, we can expect the reaction of women poets to the floral to be varied and contradictory, especially in poems reflecting on female sexuality. Some women poets use flowers to refer to women in terms equally derogatory as those employed by men. For example, Anna Seward's 'Sonnet. To the Poppy' (1799) compares the 'flimsy, showy, melancholy weed' to a 'love-crazed maid'. Other poets, such as Christina Rossetti, turn to flowers as an effective means of voicing the painful consequences of sexual attractiveness for women. In 'The Solitary Rose', a poem written when she was seventeen (1847), Rossetti suggests that the flower is happiest when secluded away from those who desire to 'mar thy beauty in a wanton hour'; whereas in 'Autumn Violets', composed two decades later (1868), she despairs when the flowers come into bloom too late and out of season.

Many women poets employ the language of flowers as a means of writing charged and subversive poems of sexual desire, most notably and influentially, Emily Dickinson. Her delightful poem about a clover, 'There Is A Flower That Bees Prefer' (*c.* 1862), is an exultant celebration of the flower's delicious desirability, written in terms of absolute confidence:

Her Public — be the Noon —
Her Providence — the Sun —
Her Progress — by the Bee — proclaimed —
In sovereign — Swerveless Tune —

In so many ways, Emily Dickinson changed the rules of poetry. Here, the centuries of negative, constrictive, petty associations made between women and small flowers are simply tossed to one side. The impact she had on women poets, especially those expressing desire in poems about flowers, is revolutionary. Dickinson's influence can be seen in the work of most women poets who followed her, not necessarily in obvious ways or perhaps even consciously, but more in terms of our unabashed confidence in tackling the terrain, of having the nerve to write 'Swerveless Tunes' about ourselves. Two of many examples you'll find in *Flora Poetica* are a poem in which Sandra McPherson comes to terms with her fiftieth birthday by comparing herself to a 'Phlox Diffusa' with its 'Taproots eight to fifteen feet' deep; And Vicki Feaver's celebration of the potency of 'Marigolds', which are 'Not the flowers men give women' but rather are 'flowers that burst / from tight, explosive buds, rayed / like the sun'.

But although women poets frequently employ flowers as metaphors for femininity and female desire, no (heterosexual) woman poet, as far as I can tell, writes *erotically* and directly about men in the way they regularly apostrophise women in 'the language of flowers'. Isabella Valancy Crawford (1850–87) surrounds a male lover with water-lilies in her extraordinary, erotic poem, 'The Lily Bed', and Kathleen Jamie's beautifully sensual Scots lyric, 'Speirin' ('Proposal') is an invitation to a man to 'whummel' (tumble) in the dusty bluebell woods, but this isn't quite the same thing. The bunch of chrysanthemums in Rita Dove's 'Then Came Flowers' is endowed with 'Plumage as proud, as cocky as firecrackers', and Denise Levertov refers to 'Brother Ivy' in generous, fraternal terms — but these are scant examples to set against the centuries of men poets comparing us to fragile blooms. Maybe I missed something (and, like all anthologists, I wake up in the middle of the night fretting over books not called up from the basement of the British Library) but it's a remarkable blind spot. Obviously this absence is a powerful indication of the embeddedness of the connections we still make between flowers and femininity. But I also suspect it's a reflection on the difficulties (heterosexual) women poets continue to face in regarding ourselves as the subject of our poems, and the men we love as the poetic objects of our desires[21].

Like women poets, men only rarely assign masculine qualities to plants. Ted Hughes' conquering 'Thistles' are resolutely male, as are John Clare's: 'proud as a war-horse'. Blake Morrison's 'Cuckoo-pint' is another exception — though here it's countered by Ted Walker's poem of the same name[22]. The mandrakes in Thom Gunn's delightful poem, as their name suggests, are one plant steeped in traditions of masculine associations. Trees, however, are another matter. Usually they are permitted a neutral, ungendered existence; more rarely they have feminine qualities; and sometimes they take on a decidedly masculine tone, such as the live-oak which makes Walt Whitman 'think of manly love'. But all these plants — thistles, cuckoo-pints, mandrakes, trees in general — are more open to masculine associations because they're prickly, hairy, phallic or imposingly large, qualities we still associate with manliness, not femininity. Unlike the rose that Fred Voss takes to work.

Poets use plants to articulate issues of power other than those of gender, and the revolutionary rose is not the only vegetable symbol they adopt. In 'The Book of Juniper' the Irish poet, Tom Paulin, admires this 'tree of freedom' for the manner in which it 'ducks its head down and skirts / the warped polities of other trees / bent in the Atlantic wind'. On the other side of the Atlantic, two African-American poets turn to plants as a means of remembering the ordeals of their people: Paul Laurence Dunbar refers to lynching in his horrifying ballad, 'The Haunted Oak' (1903), whereas Jean Toomer, writing just as the Harlem Renaissance got underway, produces a tender, more hopeful poem in 'November Cotton Flower' (1923). The blossoms of the jacaranda tree explode when trodden underfoot, and it's this sound that two African poets employ to comment on episodes of political violence: the South African poet, Lionel Abrahams, refers to the atrocities committed in Soweto in 'After Winter '76', while Jack Mapanje, from Malawi, writes about escaping from the despotism of Hastings Banda's regime in 'Seasoned Jacarandas'. In 'The Acacias of Gabarone City, Botswana' Jack Mapanje reminds us of the contingency of symbols, reflecting on the irony of once having flinched at trees, 'shattered by the cruel bombs of apartheid' which are now being planted by a friend to protect his own private property.

But it's the subject of colonialism, of the history of the British Empire growing in gardens across the English-speaking world (wherever and however we may plant them[23]) that inevitably is a main concern of many of the poems I've collected here. A few poets, as we've seen, address the subject of colonial transplantation directly. But what I've found particularly fascinating is how poets from all over the English-speaking world repeatedly turn to their indigenous flora as subject matter, an interesting parallel to the way in which some women poets use the traditional language of flowers to assert their own independent identities. In this case these post-colonial poets use their local flora as a subtle means of identifying their 'roots', of asserting their special, particular place in the world — much as John Clare was doing in rural England during the early nineteenth century.

The impulse for this poetic assertiveness springs from Romanticism, from its stress on individual, particular identity and from the enormous significance the natural world had for poets of the period. Romanticism crossed the Atlantic to America in the writings of Ralph Waldo Emerson (1803–82) who met Coleridge and Wordsworth during his tour of Europe in 1832–33. On returning home he published *Nature*, a work which stressed the transcendental importance of the natural world and accorded special importance to American natural phenomena. *Nature* had an immense influence on generations of writers to come, both in America and beyond. Emerson's poem about a local shrub, 'The Rhodora', was written in 1834, just after he met the great Romantic poets and when he had already begun working on his book. Emerson's most renowned disciple, Walt Whitman (1819–92), famously celebrated all that was specific to America, as in his poem 'I Saw in Louisiana a Live-Oak Growing' (1860); I've also included Emily Dickinson's poem about a hemlock spruce (*c.* 1862), both trees being species native to North America. Throughout the twentieth century, Canadian and American poets have carried on this tradition of writing about their indigenous flora, among them Hart Crane, Eric Ormsby, Margaret Atwood, Adrienne Rich and, especially, Louise Glück and Amy Clampitt.

The first major Indian poet to write in English was Toru Dutt (1856–77), whose death at twenty-one deprived poetry in English, and her homeland, of a major talent. Dutt was profoundly influenced by Romantic poets, especially John Keats, as one of her greatest poems, 'Our Casuarina Tree' (1882), indicates so clearly. That possessive in the title refers not only to the beautiful tree growing in her family's garden, but also to the obvious pride she took in the beautiful surroundings of her native Bengal.

Poets from Britain's former colonies continued to celebrate their local flora throughout the twentieth century. As many countries struggled for independence from Britain, particularly during the period after the Second World War, this inspired a new confidence and pride in indigenous traditions and cultures, confidence which in turn fuelled the various liberation movements throughout the former British Empire. These political upheavals, combined with the growing influence of the conservation movement active since the 'sixties, have led to an increasing importance being placed on the preservation of local, often endangered, species of flora and their surrounding environments[24].

In *Flora Poetica* you will find lignum vitae, sea-almonds and starapples from the Caribbean in the poems of Edward Baugh, Derek Walcott and Olive Senior, and a magnificent tamarind tree which the Jamaican poet, Lorna Goodison, uses to encapsulate a history of her people. Like Lorna Goodison, the Australian poet, Oodgeroo Noonuccal, also turns to a tree, this time a battered municipal gum-tree, to reflect on the circumstances her people have endured. She shares the eucalyptus family, Myrtaceae, with the great Australian poet, Les Murray, who writes poems about a eucalyptus tree and '*Angophora floribunda*', which the homesick English colonisers called 'apples' to make the plant seem more familiar. Another major Australian poet particularly drawn to botany is Judith Wright, who here examines cycads, a phaius orchid and a flame-tree, all of which are native to Australia. In New Zealand, James K Baxter considers the local Ngaio tree, Ruth Dallas tries living with a Cabbage-tree, and Chris Orsman writes about ornamental gorse, a plant which has turned into an appalling pest, disfiguring the local landscape having been transplanted to New Zealand from its home by British colonial settlers.

The gorse plant is also the subject of poems by two poets from Britain's first venture into colonialist exploitation, Ireland, who consider the shrub more favourably in its native habitat. Seamus Heaney calls gorse by its local name of 'whin' in his poem 'Whinlands'; in the poem, Heaney mentions how if you 'Put a match under whins / They go up of a sudden', a theme which Michael Longley also explores in his beautiful lyric, 'Gorse Fires'.

Michael Longley has often paid tribute to the influence John Clare has had on his delicate, patient poems about botany. And reading all these poets celebrating the particulars of their indigenous flora reminds me of the pioneering endeavours of Clare and his close attention to the common flowers of a nineteenth-century Northamptonshire parish. Sadly, Clare's poems barely found an audience during his lifetime — especially in the Victorian period when they were seen as much too crude — but his poetry reads remarkably freshly to us now. Clare's way of examining nature and of writing almost observational notes, largely bare of metapor or symbols and free of abstractions, chimes so well with the guiding principles of Modernism. 'No ideas but in Things', wrote William Carlos Williams, and 'Go in fear of abstractions' commanded Ezra Pound and, by and large throughout the last century, we did.

It's Modernism's insistence of the primacy of the object in the poem which partly explains why there were so many poems written about plants and flowers during the twentieth century. But I think we also should note how fashionable gardens, gardening and flowers have become, especially in Britain during the past two decades, and no longer only for the rich. Because of growing prosperity, at least for some people, gardening has become an increasingly popular pastime, and flowers are more visible in Britain nowadays — even if they're not grown here but are shipped in from places like Gaza, Zimbabwe or Brazil. Many poets in *Flora Poetica* examine plants now common throughout the temperate world in gardens or as houseplants: gentians, lilies, geraniums, acacias, gardenias, orchids, marigolds, ginkgoes, hydrangeas, cyclamens and the amaryllis, to name but a few. And many poets, notably D. H. Lawrence and Sylvia Plath, turn to cut flowers to particularly startling effect.

The familiarity which many of us now have with a far greater number of different plants is reflected in the variety of species used as subject matter by contemporary poets. Poems written before the twentieth century only account for 25 of the 76 plant families represented here[25]. Many of these 'new' plants and plant families occur when poets, especially those living outside Britain, examine local plants in their native settings. Others belong to the travelling exotics which have taken complex journeys across the globe, found new homes and become part of the scenery: for example, the jacaranda trees to which Jack Mapanje and Lionel Abrahams so easily refer are not actually native to southern Africa, but are imports from Argentina.

Since *Flora Poetica* is an anthology inevitably and profoundly concerned with the transplantation of plants, it's also equally involved with the transplantation of poets, poetry and the English language[27]. Poets from all over the world have turned to poetry in order to describe the routes they have travelled, the roots they have set down, or the roots and routes they've lost. That they do so through the imagery of plants — through the language of flowers — adds to the poignancy and beauty of the poems they've created, especially when we come to understand the many long and varied journeys the poems, the poets and the plants themselves have taken to find us waiting here.

As a wet and frozen teenager with blistered hands, knee-deep in leaf-mould towards the end of yet another back-breaking Wednesday afternoon in mid-February, I used to wonder where all this would get me. Now I know. At the time, of course, I couldn't possibly have imagined being absorbed in a project as wonderful as *Flora Poetica*. Nor did I know much about the complex histories of the numerous plants that were passing through my muddy grasp. And, even up till very recently, a large number of the poems and poets I've collected here remained unknown to me. In so many different ways, editing this anthology has been a revelation. I can only hope that reading *Flora Poetica* brings you some of the immense delight I have found in discovering these poets, attempting to understand the background to their poems, and unravelling the stories of the plants that they've addressed.

1 My poems about plants and gardens can be found in *The Florist's at Midnight*, (London; Jonathan Cape, 2001).

2 My residency at Chelsea, as well as the work of other poets in gardens, is described in the collection of essays I've edited, *A Green Thought in a Green Shade: Poetry in the Garden* (London; The Poetry Society, 2000).

3 Penelope Hobhouse, *Plants in Garden History* (London; Pavilion, 1992) pp. 96–98. I owe an enormous debt to this fascinating book.

4 See Anna Pavord, *The Tulip* (London; Bloomsbury, 1999).

5 Joseph Addison, *The Spectator No. 69* (Saturday, 19 May 1711).

6 See Richard Drayton *Nature's Government: Science, Imperial Britain, and the 'Improvement' of the World* (New Haven and London; Yale University Press, 2000) for by far the best account of the relationship between colonialism and horticulture; also Jane Brown, *The Pursuit of Paradise: A Social History of Gardens and Gardening* (London; HarperCollins, 1999) chapter 6, 'Acquiring Eden'.

7 See Michael Leapman's *The Ingenious Mr Fairchild: The Forgotten Father of the Flower Garden* (London; Headline, 2000) for an account of the rapid increase in London plant nurseries during the early eighteenth century.

8 See Henry Hobhouse, *Seeds of Change: Six Plants that Transformed Mankind*

(new edition, London; Macmillan, 1999); and Toby & Will Musgrave, *An Empire of Plants: People and Plants that Changed the World* (London; Cassell, 2000).

9 Toby Musgrave, Chris Gardener and Will Musgrave, *The Plant Hunters: Two Hundred Years of Adventure and Discovery Around the World* (London; Ward Lock, 1998) p. 53. As well as collecting beautiful plants, botany could also 'provide a cover for espionage', and 'The botanical exploration of the Cape by Masson provided information useful to its seizure by Britain', Drayton (*op. cit.*) p. 111.

10 The marigold's origins remain unclear, though it is mentioned by the first-century Latin poet, Columella. Hobhouse (*op. cit.*) p. 25.

11 According to the *Oxford English Dictionary*, the term 'botany' ('the science which treats of plants') is first recorded in 1696.

12 See Martin Kemp, '"Implanted in our Natures": humans, plants and the stories of art' in David Philip Miller and Peter Hanns Reill (eds.) *Visions of Empire: Voyages, Botany and Representations of Nature* (Cambridge; Cambridge University Press, 1996) pp. 197–229, and Celia Fisher, *Pocket Guides: Flowers and Fruit* (London; National Gallery Publications, 1998).

13 See Richard Mabey, *Flora Britannica* (London; Chatto & Windus, 1997) for a rich and fascinating account of the traditional meanings of plants.

14 See Ann B. Shteir, *Cultivating Women, Cultivating Science: Flora's Daughters and Botany in England 1760–1860* (Baltimore; Johns Hopkins University Press, 1996) for a fascinating account of how women were able to make significant contributions to the early developments of eighteenth-century botany before the attempt to turn it into a 'proper' (masculine) science around 1830.

15 Shelley's 'Sensitive Plant' is another exclusion: despite its title, the poem's focus is a garden and the many plants it contains, rather than *Mimosa pudica* itself.

16 Ann B. Shteir, (*op. cit.*) p. 21. The Wordsworths' handbook was the third edition of *A Botanical Arrangement of All the Vegetables Naturally Growing in Great Britain* by William Withering, first published in 1776.

17 This 'renaming' of the natural world by botanists can be seen as part of the project of colonial possession since the plants themselves already had perfectly good names as far as indigenous peoples were concerned. As Jamaica Kincaid writes, 'these new plants from far away, like the people far away, had no history, no names, and so they could be given names.' Jamaica Kincaid *My Garden (book)*: (London; Vintage, 2000) p. 91; from her article, 'To Name is to Possess'.

18 The common names of plant families, like the common names of plants themselves, are something of a movable feast. As Ericaceae contains both heathers and rhododendrons, it would be perfectly correct (though not common practice, at least as far as I'm aware) to call it 'the rhododendron family'.

19 See Mark Doty's 'Lilacs in NYC' in *Sweet Machine* (London; Jonathan Cape, 1998) pp. 89–91 — another poem I'm hoping to include in my garden poems anthology.

20 There's a vast, and ever-increasing, number of books and articles about this subject. For an accessible introduction I'd recommend Roger Lonsdale's lucid Introduction to his anthology of *Eighteenth-Century Women Poets* (Oxford; Oxford University Press, 1989). For an account from a poet's perspective see Adrienne Rich's groundbreaking essay, 'When We Dead Awaken' (1971), widely reprinted, most recently in her *Arts of the Possible: Essays and Conversations* (New York, London; Norton & Co, 2001).

21 See my essay, 'Dilemmas and Developments: Eavan Boland Re-examined' in *Feminist Review* No. 62, Summer 1999, pp. 58–66.

22 I've followed these two poems by Michael Longley's 'Self-heal' — which, if ordered according to its title would be placed in Labiatae, the mint family — because the drama in the poem centres around the day the speaker of the poem, 'pulled a cuckoo-pint apart'.

23 Richard Drayton points out that wilderness is 'a kind of land use', and that 'Green' ideas of conservation and preservation are imbricated within colonialist notions of cultivation. Drayton (*op. cit.*) p. 235; chapters 1 & 7 *passim.*

24 The title of a leaflet written by Dawn Sanders and Sue Minter of Chelsea Physic Garden — *Rare Plants, Endangered Peoples, Lost Knowledge* — sums up both the devastating effects which follow from the destruction of fragile environments, and the absolute interdependence of culture and flora.

25 It's worth bearing in mind this isn't an exhaustive empirical survey of all poems about plants written by all poets everywhere in English, and of course other plants feature in pre-twentieth century poems that I've not included.

26 Given how deeply this book is absorbed with botany, colonialism and transplantation, it's been particularly important to me to include poets from all over the English-speaking world. I've excluded poems in translation — with one exception: I hadn't realised Sir Richard Fanshawe's 'A Rose' was a translation (from the Spanish of Góngora) until it was far too bedded down in the text to uproot it.

Textual Matters

Although the poems in the book are not arranged chronologically, I think it is important to know when they were first published. This is the date you'll find (in italics) after each poem. Where two dates are given in italics, the second refers to a published version that differs in an important way from the first. Where the date of composition differs significantly from the publication date, and is known (or can reasonably be inferred), I've given that too: before the publication date (in roman type).

As far as possible, I've used the first published edition of a poem. This means that I've kept archaic and inconsistent spellings, though I've not gone as far as using the 'long s' or 'v' for 'u'.

The botanical authority I've relied upon in order to name the plants and arrange the poems is D. J. Mabberley, *The Plant-Book: A Portable Dictionary of the Vascular Plants*, second (corrected) edition (Cambridge; Cambridge University Press, 1998). Mabberley differs from other sources used by gardeners in Britain – referring to the daisy family as Compositae not Asteraceae, and the grass family as Gamineae not Poaceae – and gardeners elsewhere may be startled to find plants they think of as being in Liliaceae moved to different families. I am extremely grateful to Sue Minter, Curator of the Chelsea Physic Garden, for her invaluable assistance with the botanical information here; any errors are my own.

Some readers will notice I've arranged the plant families alphabetically, rather than using the system for the arrangement of vascular plants introduced by Bentham and Hooker in the nineteenth century. It was the wonderful poems I'd collected about plants in Amaryllidaceae which made me decide on alphabetical ordering: under the system, as monocotyledons, they'd have appeared right near the end of the book.

In the notes to the poems I have given the botanical names of the plants and where they originate the first time that a particular species occurs. Likewise, in the Index of Poets, I have noted where the poets are from. When a poet has ended up living for most of his or her life somewhere other than their birth-country, I have indicated that too — though some poets, particularly the wandering Modernists, have defeated me, and you will have to forgive me for truncating their journeys.

Aceraceae: Maple family

John Clare

The Maple Tree

The maple with its tassel flowers of green,
That turns to red a staghorn-shaped seed,
Just spreading out its scolloped leaves is seen,
Of yellowish hue, yet beautifully green;
Bark ribbed like corderoy in seamy screed,
That farther up the stem is smoother seen,
Where the white hemlock with white umbel flowers
Up each spread stoven to the branches towers;
And moss around the stoven spreads, dark green,
And blotched leaved orchis, and the blue bell flowers;
Thickly they grow and neath the leaves are seen;
I love to see them gemmed with morning hours,
I love the lone green places where they be,
And the sweet clothing of the maple tree.

(1842–64, *1920*)

Acer campestre
field or hedge maple

Europe, including Britain

Marianne Moore

The Sycamore

Against a gun-metal sky
I saw an albino giraffe. Without
leaves to modify,
chamois-white as
said, although partly pied near the base,
it towered where a chain of
stepping-stones lay in a stream nearby;
glamor to stir the envy

of anything in motley —
Hampshire pig, the living lucky-stone; or
all-white butterfly.
A commonplace:
there's more than just one kind of grace.
We don't like flowers that do
not wilt; they must die, and nine
she-camel-hairs aid memory.

Worthy of Imami,
the Persian — clinging to a stiffer stalk
was a little dry
thing from the grass,
in the shape of a Maltese cross,
retiringly formal
as if to say: 'And there was I
like a field-mouse at Versailles.'

(*1956*)

Acer pseudoplatanus
sycamore

Europe, West Asia

William Carlos Williams

Young Sycamore

I must tell you
this young tree
whose round and firm trunk
between the wet

pavement and the gutter
(where water
is trickling) rises
bodily

into the air with
one undulant
thrust half its height —
and then

dividing and waning
sending out
young branches on
all sides —

hung with cocoons
it thins
till nothing is left of it
but two

eccentric knotted
twigs
bending forward
hornlike at the top

(*1934*)

Agavaceae: Agave family

Jamie McKendrick

The Century Plant

A century after its introduction
to Oxford's Botanical Gardens greenhouse,
on the site of the medieval Jewish cemetery,
the agave has taken a leap of faith
it won't survive, and begun to blaze
with sulphurous buds. It's not clear whether
global or more local warming lit the fuse
in the patient rootstock and sent one limb
rocketing upward so its top
can look down even on the banana tree
besides the other transplants. The palm-line
is said to move a metre north each year
— these days more like a kilometre —
but either way the agave's too far ahead
to be caught up with, despite the hundred years
of waiting — now two, at the most three weeks
of prodigal flowering and the whole thing ends.

In 1850 in Seville,
while his contemporaries photographed
rotting barges on the Guadalquivir
or farm labourers in sheepskin waistcoats
or Gypsy women in the tobacco factory,
Victome J. de Vigier,
turned his back on the folkloric and his lens
on the common-or-garden naturalized exotics
like palm trees and bamboo. His masterpiece,
Etude d'aloès, shows this tumid
dusty plant on a nondescript roadside.
It holds grimly on to its patch of nowhere
and drinks and drinks the silver nitrate light
as though there were no belonging anywhere

but there and then, and nothing sublime
except that stretch of dirt, that broken wall
and the rays of a faded nineteenth-century sun.

(*1997*)

Agave americana
century plant

East Mexico

Alliaceae: Onion family

Myrna Stone

Wild Onion

In botany, *Allium stellatum*, of the family
Alliaceae, cousin to trillium, Solomon's-seal
and bellwort, whose root, bulb, leaf and stem

are edible or medicinal; fodder for squirrel,
elk, deer, poultice for boils, anodyne for fever,
sting of bee and wasp, amulet to ward off

dizziness or croup — from the Old French
oignon, and the Latin *unio*, meaning oneness —
organism of obfuscation and trumpery

whose lavender blossoms deftly belie
the flagrant acidic breath that draws us
now, step-by-step, up from the river's bank

to its grassy open bed. Siren of the olfactory —
most evocative of the senses — its leaves
bristle and flare, summoning to each of us

a summer kitchen, and in it, a mother, aproned
and dewy, weeping at her chopping block . . .
But we are, after all, animal, and what seduces

here, in the shank of the day, is vegetable:
a booty we will dig for like dogs and take home
for our supper, a shill, a shindy, a caustic pearl.

(*2001*)

Allium stellatum
wild onion

North America

Amaryllidaceae: Daffodil family

James Lasdun

Timing

The secret of good comedy. Ours was bad,
A hot-house passion blooming under force
of imminent separation. Were our eyes
Bigger than our hearts? A candlebud
Of amaryllis burned for you in my room
Three thousand miles away. You stalled your visit
Twice, mysteriously, and came too late.
Our out-of-sync phone calls were a bad dream —
Echolocation of love! My lopped bromeliad's
Adze-stumps turned to black bronze as you rode
The planet into light, five hours ahead.
Even when you came we lived in shifts,
Watching the amaryllis' oxblood explode;
Ten days of brilliance, then abruptly dead.

(*1995*)

Amaryllis belladonna
belladonna lily

Republic of South Africa

Jorie Graham

Opulence

The self-brewing of the amaryllis rising before me.
Weeks of something's decomposing — like hearsay
growing — into this stringent self-analysis —
a tyranny of utter self-reflexiveness —
its nearness to the invisible a deep fissure
the day suck round as its frontiers trill, slur
— a settling-ever-upward and then,
now,
this utterly sound-free-though-tongued opening
where some immortal scale is screeched —
bits of *clench, jolt, fray* and *assuage* —
bits of *gnaw* and *pulse* and, even, *ruse*
— impregnable dribble — wingbeat at a speed
too slow to see — stepping out of the casing outstretched,
high-heeled —
something from underneath coaxing the packed buds up,
loosening their perfect fit — the smooth skin between them
striating then
beginning to wrinkle and fold
so as to loosen the tight dictation of the four inseparable polished
and bullioned
buds — color seeping-up till the icy green releases the sensation of
a set of reds
imprisoned in it, flushed, though not yet truly
visible — the green still starchy — clean —
till the four knots grow loose in their armor,
and the two dimensions of their perfect-fit fill out and a third,
shadow, seeps in
loosening and loosening,
and the envelope rips,
and the fringes slip off and begin to fray at their newly freed
tips,
and the enameled, vaulting, perfectly braided
Immaculate
is jostled, unpacked —
the force, the phantom, now sending armloads up
into the exclamation,

and the skin marbles, and then, when I look again,
has already begun to speckle, then blush, then a solid un-
avoidable incarnadine,
the fourness of it now maneuvering, vitalized,
like antennae rearranging constantly,
the monologue reduced — or is it expanded — to
this chatter seeking all the bits of light,
the four of them craning this way then that according to
the time
of day, the drying wrinkled skirts of the casing
now folded-down beneath, formulaic,
the light wide-awake around it — or is it the eye —
yes yes yes yes says the mechanism of the underneath tick
tock —
and no footprints to or from the place —
no footprints to or from —

(*1996*)

Anna Laetitia Barbauld

The Snowdrop

Already now the snowdrop dares appear,
The first pale blossom of th'unripen'd year;
As Flora's breath, by some transforming power,
Had chang'd an icicle into a flower,
Its name and hue the scentless plant retains,
And winter lingers in its icy veins.

(*c.* 1766, *1835*)

Galanthus nivalis
Snowdrop

Europe, naturalised in Britain and Ireland

Louise Glück

Snowdrops

Do you know what I was, how I lived? You know
what despair is; then
winter should have meaning for you.

I did not expect to survive,
earth suppressing me. I didn't expect
to waken again, to feel
in damp earth my body
able to respond again, remembering
after so long how to open again
in the cold light
of earliest spring —

afraid, yes, but among you again
crying yes risk joy

in the raw wind of the new world.

(*1992*)

Ted Hughes

Snowdrop

Now is the globe shrunk tight
Round the mouse's dulled wintering heart.
Weasel and crow, as if moulded in brass,
Move through an outer darkness
Not in their right minds,
With the other deaths. She, too, pursues her ends,
Brutal as the stars of this month,
Her pale head heavy as metal.

(*1960*)

Lauris Edmond

Jonquils

(*For Kathy*)

I remember the cold slide of my hands
on the stalks down, down to the locked knot
where each green column began;

and the wrenching, the slithering grip
till it bent over, slipped, came
at last (perhaps pulling up buried inches

from deep in the ground); then the adding
of huge handfuls to the heap at the edge,
while a strong sweetness flooded

our faces, sap dropped its cold syrup
on our feet and the wind swirled in the trees.
It was August, the spring of every year

of our lives was there on that slippery
bank as we gathered the white armfuls,
shouting in the wind and laughing,

taking with us the whole sappy morning,
a delicate load, to put in glass jars
on tables in kitchens all across the world.

(*1997*)

Narcissus jonquilla
jonquil

South-west Europe, naturalised elsewhere

Nora Hopper (later Chesson)

Two Women

You are a snowdrop, sweet; but will
You look upon this daffodil
That in a careless hand has lain
So long, it cannot drink the rain
And be renewed, or by the sun
Find that unkindly grasp undone?

You are a snowdrop: put your white
By the spoiled gold, dear heart, to-night:
Touch leaves with this less happy flower
Undone by some too happy hour.
You might have been the daffodil
If I had kissed your prudence still.

(*1900*)

Robert Herrick

To Daffadills

Faire Daffadills, we weep to see
You haste away so soone:
As yet the early-rising Sun
Has not attain'd his Noone.
Stay, stay,
Untill the hasting day
Has run
But to the Even-song;
And, having pray'd together, we
Will goe with you along.

2. We have short time to stay, as you,
We have as short a Spring;
As quick a growth to meet Decay,
As you, or any thing.
We die,
As your hours doe, and drie
Away,
Like to the Summeres raine;
Or as the pearles of Mornings dew,
Ne'er to be found again.

(*1648*)

Narcissus pesudonarcissus
wild daffodil, Lent lily, Tenby daffodil

Europe

Sylvia Plath

Among the Narcissi

Spry, wry, and gray as these March sticks,
Percy bows, in his blue peajacket, among the narcissi.
He is recuperating from something on the lung.

The narcissi, too, are bowing to some big thing:
It rattles their stars on the green hill where Percy
Nurses the hardship of his stitches, and walks and walks.

There is a dignity to this; there is a formality —
The flowers vivid as bandages, and the man mending.
They bow and stand: they suffer such attacks!

And the octogenarian loves the little flocks.
He is quite blue; the terrible wind tries his breathing.
The narcissi look up like children, quickly and whitely.

(1962, *1971*)

Ted Hughes

Daffodils

Remember how we picked the daffodils?
Nobody else remembers, but I remember.
Your daughter came with her armfuls, eager and happy,
Helping the harvest. She has forgotten.
She cannot even remember you. And we sold them.
It sounds like sacrilege, but we sold them.
Were we so poor? Old Stoneman, the grocer,
Boss-eyed, his blood-pressure purpling to beetroot
(It was his last chance,
He would die in the same great freeze as you),
He persuaded us. Every Spring
He always bought them, sevenpence a dozen,
'A custom of the house'.

Besides, we still weren't sure we wanted to own
Anything. Mainly we were hungry
To convert everything to profit.
Still nomads — still strangers
To our whole possession. The daffodils
Were incidental gilding of the deeds,
Treasure trove. They simply came,
And they kept on coming.
As if not from the sod but falling from heaven.
Our lives were still a raid on our own good luck.
We knew we'd live for ever. We had not learned
What a fleeting glance of the everlasting
Daffodils are. Never identified
The nuptial flight of the rarest ephemera —
Our own days!
                    We thought they were a windfall.
Never guessed they were a last blessing.
So we sold them. We worked at selling them
As if employed on someone else's
Flower-farm. You bent at it
In the rain of that April — your last April.
We bent there together, among the soft shrieks
Of their jostled stems, the wet shocks shaken
Of their girlish dance frocks —

Fresh-opened dragonflies, wet and flimsy,
Opened too early.

We piled their frailty lights on a carpenter's bench,
Distributed leaves among the dozens —
Buckling blade-leaves, limber, groping for air, zinc-silvered —
Propped their raw butts in bucket water,
Their oval, meaty butts,
And sold them, sevenpence a bunch —

Wind-wounds, spasms from the dark earth,
With their odourless metals,
A flamy purification of the deep grave's stony cold
As if ice had a breath —

We sold them, to wither.
The crop thickened faster than we could thin it.
Finally, we were overwhelmed
And we lost our wedding-present scissors.

Every March since they have lifted again
Out of the same bulbs, the same
Baby-cries from the thaw,
Ballerinas too early for music, shiverers
In the draughty wings of the year.
On that same groundswell of memory, fluttering
They return to forget you stooping there
Behind the rainy curtains of a dark April,
Snipping their stems.

But somewhere your scissors remember. Wherever they are.
Here somewhere, blades wide open,
April by April
Sinking deeper
Through the sod — an anchor, a cross of rust.

(*1998*)

William Wordsworth

'I Wandered Lonely as a Cloud'

I wandered lonely as a Cloud
That floats on high o'er Vales and Hills,
When all at once I saw a crowd,
A host, of golden Daffodils;
Beside the Lake, beneath the trees,
Fluttering and dancing in the breeze.

Continuous as the stars that shine
And twinkle on the milky way,
They stretched in never-ending line
Along the margin of a bay:
Ten thousand saw I at a glance,
Tossing their heads in sprightly dance.

The waves beside them danced; but they
Out-did the sparkling waves in glee:
A Poet could not but be gay
In such a jocund company:
I gazed — and gazed — but little thought
What wealth the shew to me had brought:

For oft, when on my couch I lie
In vacant or in pensive mood,
They flash upon that inward eye
Which is the bliss of solitude,
And then my heart with pleasure fills,
And dances with the Daffodils.

(*1807*, *1815*)

Michael Longley

The Daffodils

Your daughter is reading to you over and over again
Wordsworth's 'The Daffodils', her lips at your ear.
She wants you to know what a good girl you have been.
You are so good at joined-up writing the page you
Have filled with your knowledge is completely black.
Your hand presses her hand in response to rhyme words.
She wants you to turn away from the wooden desk
Before you die, and look out of the classroom window
Where all the available space is filled with daffodils.

(*2000*)

Aquifoliaceae: Holly family

A. R. Ammons

Holly

The hollybush flowers
small whites (become of
course berries)
four tiny petals
turned
back and four
anthers stuck out:
the pistil low &
honey-high:
wasp-bees (those small
wasps or
bees) come around
with a glee too
fine to hear: when
the wind dies
at dusk, silence,
unaffronted,
puts a robe
slightly thinner
than sight over
all the flowers
so darkness &
the terrible stars
will not hurt them.

(*1986*)

Ilex aquifolium
holly, prickbush

Europe and the Mediterranean

Peter Redgrove

Of Prickbush

Most archaic plant, or prickbush, the holly,
Bluish-green when immature,
The sheen of corpses as they start to travel
The insect-path, colour
Of duality, the ocean and the sky.

There is much holly on these quarry cliffs,
Blocks of dynamited stone, rusty rails
Like stitched wounds, and the trees which prise
More stone with their slow green dynamitings,
And the west gulf packed with prickbush.
An apple-tree fruits at the whiskery lip,
A shower of fruit falls
Into the holly-bushes where the birds find refuge
In their dark green attics;
Separated by the prickly walls, these birds
Become individuals and sing for themselves, yet chime.

Most archaic plant, the mother holly
Is the first house, her doll of holly wood
The kern baby, signifying the seed
Or kernel of future harvest,
And the heaven at the centre of the tree
Where the birds sing
Like the repeaters of life
And nest in the prickly dark land of song.

(*1989*)

Araceae: Arum family

Blake Morrison

Cuckoo-pint

A brown matchstick held up in the wind,
the bract-leaf cupped around it like a palm.

March had not extinguished it: there it lurked,
sly as something done behind the sheds,

slithering from its half-unrolled umbrella
as we snipped pussy-willow from the lanes.

To come instead on this old man of the woods,
tanned and cowled and clammed inside his collar,

his shirt-front splattered with tobacco stains,
his poker oozy with tuber-froth,

was like learning by accident a secret
intended for later, exciting

and obscene and not to be gone back on,
like the knowledge of atoms, or death.

(*1999*)

Arum maculatum
cuckoo-pint, Jack-in-the-pulpit, lords-and-ladies, wake robin

Europe

Ted Walker

Cuckoo-Pint

So cold now. I remember
you — bright hedgerow tarts you were,
flagrant in your big red beads,
cheerful, vulgar and brazen.
But then

in a sudden October
when the white night of winter
came, you put aside your gauds
and took vows. Now you open
again,

hooded, cool and sinister.
I know you for what you are
unveiled: loose, secular brides
frustrated with this convent
torment.

(*1965*)

Michael Longley

Self-heal

I wanted to teach him the names of flowers,
Self-heal and centaury; on the long acre
Where cattle never graze, bog asphodel.
Could I love someone so gone in the head
And, as they say, was I leading him on?
He'd slept in the cot until he was twelve
Because of his babyish ways, I suppose,
Or the lack of a bed: hadn't his father
Gambled away all but rushy pasture?
His skull seemed to be hammered like a wedge
Into his shoulders, and his back was hunched,
Which gave him an almost scholarly air.
But he couldn't remember the things I taught:
Each name would hover above its flower
Like a butterfly unable to alight.
That day I pulled a cuckoo-pint apart
To release the giddy insects from their cell.
Gently he slipped his hand between my thighs.
I wasn't frightened; and still I don't know why,
But I ran from him in tears to tell them.
I heard how every day for one whole week
He was flogged with a blackthorn, then tethered
In the hayfield. I might have been the cow
Whose tail he would later dock with shears,
And he the ram tangled in barbed wire
That he stoned to death when they set him free.

(*1979*)

Prunella vulgaris
Labiatae (Mint family)
self-heal

Eurasia

(See 'Introduction', footnote n.22, p.xxxiv)

Eric Ormsby

Skunk Cabbage

The skunk cabbage with its smug and opulent smell
Opens in plump magnificence near the edge
Of garbage-strewn canals, or you see its shape
Arise near the wet roots of the marsh.
How vigilant it looks with its glossy leaves
Parted to disclose its bruised insides,
That troubled purple of its blossom!
It always seemed so squat, dumpy and rank,
A noxious efflorescence of the swamp,
Until I got down low and looked at it.
Now I search out its blunt totemic shape
And bow when I see its outer stalks
Drawn aside, like the frilly curtains of the ark,
For the foul magenta of its gorgeous heart.

(*1992*)

Symplocarpus foetidus
skunk cabbage, squaw lily, stink lily, chocolate lily

North-east North America

Margaret Atwood

Squaw Lilies: Some Notes

Went up the steep stone hill, thinking,
My trick hip could fail me. Went up anyway
to see the flower with three names:
chocolate lilies, for the color,
stink lilies for the smell, red meat going off,
squaw lilies. Thought what I would be like, falling.
Brain spilled on the rocks.
Said to her: never seen these before. Why squaw?
Oh, she said, something to do
with the smell.
When she said that I felt as if painted
naked on an off-blue sofa
by a bad expressionist, ochre
and dirty greens, lips thickened with yellow
pigment, a red-infected
crevice dividing the splayed legs.
Thought: this is what it is, to be part
of the landscape. Subject to
depiction. Thought:
release the lilies. They have nothing
to do with these names for them.
Not even lilies.
Went down the steep stone hill. Did not fall.

(*1986*)

Araliaceae: Ivy family

John Clare

To the Ivy

Dark creeping Ivy, with thy berries brown,
  That fondly twists' on ruins all thine own,
Old spire-points studding with a leafy crown
  Which every minute threatens to dethrone;
With fearful eye I view thy height sublime,
  And oft with quicker step retreat from thence
Where thou, in weak defiance, striv'st with Time,
  And holdst his weapons in a dread suspense.
But, bloom of ruins, thou art dear to me,
  When, far from danger's way, thy gloomy pride
Wreathes picturesque around some ancient tree
  That bows his branches by some fountain-side:
Then sweet is it from summer suns to be,
With thy green darkness overshadowing me.

(1819–21, *1821*)

Hedera helix
ivy

Mediterranean, west Asia

Denise Levertov

Brother Ivy

Between road and sidewalk, the broadleafed ivy,
unloved, dusty, littered, sanctuary of rats,
gets on with its life. New leaves shine gaily
among dogged older ones
that have lost their polish.
It does not require appreciation. The foliage
conceals a brown tangle of stems
thick as a mangrove swamp; the roots
are spread tenaciously. Unwatered
throughout the long droughts, it simply
grips the dry ground by the scruff of the neck.

I am not its steward.
If we are siblings, and I
my brother's keeper therefore,
the relation is reciprocal. The ivy
meets its obligation by pure
undoubtable being.

(*1989*)

Asclepiadaceae: Milkweed family

Philip Levine

Milkweed

Remember how unimportant
they seemed, growing loosely
in the open fields we crossed
on the way to school. We
would carve wooden swords
and slash at the luscious trunks
until the white milk started
and then flowed. Then we'd
go on to the long day after
day of the History of History
or the tables of numbers and order
as the clock slowly paid
out the moments. The windows
went dark first with rain
and then snow, and then the days,
then the years ran together and not
one mattered more than
another, and not one mattered.

Two days ago I walked
the empty woods, bent over,
crunching through oak leaves,
asking myself questions
without answers. From somewhere
a froth of seeds drifted by touched

with gold in the last light
of a lost day, going with
the wind as they always did.

(*1979*)

Asclepias spp.
milkweed

North and Central America

Asparagaceae: Asparagus family

Tom Paulin

Sparrowgrass

Though it's different from goosegrass
to say it corrupts
from out *asparagus*
would be wrong
and though sparrows
don't like to be seen in long grass
sparrowgrass is its own concept
light and wavy like the smoky bush
that grows and grows
into a soft flumy
a feathery delicacy
when you let that strange
Greek or Roman head
drive its roots deeply
into a rich gritty bed

(*1994*)

Asparagus officinalis
garden asparagus, sparrowgrass

Europe to North Africa

Balsaminaceae: Balsam family

Anne Stevenson

Himalayan Balsam

Orchid-lipped, loose-jointed, purplish, indolent flowers,
with a ripe smell of peaches, like a girl's breath through lipstick,
delicate and coarse in the weedlap of late summer rivers,
dishevelled, weak-stemmed, common as brambles, as love which

subtracts us from seasons, their courtships and murders,
(*Meta segmentata* in her web, and the male waiting,
between blossom and violent blossom, meticulous spiders
repeated in gossamer, and the slim males waiting . . .)

Fragrance too rich for keeping, too light to remember,
like grief for the cat's sparrow and the wild gull's
beach-hatched embryo. (She ran from the reaching water
with the broken egg in her hand, but the clamped bill

refused brandy and grubs, a shred too naked and perilous for
life offered freely in cardboard boxes, little windowsill
coffins for bird death, kitten death, squirrel death, summer
repeated and ended in heartbreak, in the sad small funerals.)

Sometimes, shaping bread or scraping potatoes for supper,
I have stood in the kitchen, transfixed by what I'd call love
if love were a whiff, a wanting for no particular lover,
no child, or baby or creature, 'Love, dear love'

I could cry to these scent-spilling ragged flowers
and mean nothing but 'no', by that word's breadth,
to their evident going, their important descent through red towering
stalks to the riverbed. It's not, as I thought, that death

creates love. More that love knows death. Therefore
tears, therefore poems, therefore the long stone sobs of cathedrals
that speak to no ferret or fox, that prevent no massacre.
(I am combing abundant leaves from these icy shallows.)

Love, it was you who said, 'Murder the killer
we have to call life and we'd be a bare planet under a dead sun.'
Then I loved you with the usual soft lust of October
that says 'yes' to the coming winter and a summoning odour of
  balsam.

(*1982*)

Impatiens glandulifera
policeman's helmet

Himalayas, naturalised in North America and Europe

Betulaceae: Birch family

Robert Frost

Birches

When I see birches bend to left and right
Across the lines of straighter darker trees,
I like to think some boy's been swinging them.
But swinging doesn't bend them down to stay
As ice-storms do. Often you must have seen them
Loaded with ice a sunny winter morning
After a rain. They click upon themselves
As the breeze rises, and turn many-colored
As the stir cracks and crazes their enamel.
Soon the sun's warmth makes them shed crystal shells
Shattering and avalanching on the snow-crust —
Such heaps of broken glass to sweep away
You'd think the inner dome of heaven had fallen.
They are dragged to the withered bracken by the load,
And they seem not to break; though once they are bowed
So low for long, they never right themselves:
You may see their trunks arching in the woods
Years afterwards, trailing their leaves on the ground
Like girls on hands and knees that throw their hair
Before them over their heads to dry in the sun.
But I was going to say when Truth broke in
With all her matter-of-fact about the ice-storm
I should prefer to have some boy bend them
As he went out and in to fetch the cows —
Some boy too far from town to learn baseball.
Whose only play was what he found himself.
Summer or winter, and could play alone.
One by one he subdued his father's trees
By riding them down over and over again
Until he took the stiffness out of them,
And not one but hung limp, not one was left
For him to conquer. He learned all there was
To learn about not launching out too soon

And so not carrying the tree away
Clear to the ground. He always kept his poise
To the top branches, climbing carefully
With the same pains you use to fill a cup
Up to the brim, and even above the brim.
Then he flung outward, feet first, with a swish,
Kicking his way down through the air to the ground.
So was I once myself a swinger of birches.
And so I dream of going back to be.
It's when I'm weary of considerations,
And life is too much like a pathless wood
Where your face burns and tickles with the cobwebs
Broken across it, and one eye is weeping
From a twig's having lashed across it open.
I'd like to get away from earth awhile
And then come back to it and begin over.
May no fate willfully misunderstand me
And half grant what I wish and snatch me away
Not to return. Earth's the right place for love:
I don't know where it's likely to go better.
I'd like to go by climbing a birch tree,
And climb black branches up a snow-white trunk
Toward heaven, till the tree could bear no more.
But dipped its top and set me down again.
That would be good both going and coming back.
One could do worse than be a swinger of birches.

(*1916*)

Betula spp.
birch

Northern hemisphere: temperate and tropical mountains

Bignoniaceae: Jacaranda family

Lionel Abrahams

After Winter '76

Jacaranda purple lends
a regal show to sunlit well-off streets,
burning and smoking among roofs,
splashed bright across gutters.
The blossoms, each a little air
sealed in a velvet trumpet,
make silent fanfares
and fall whole.
They burst underfoot as we pass.
Predicting their tough seeded legacy,
history should make something
of their present soft reports.

(*1984*)

Jacaranda mimosifolia
jacaranda

North-west Argentina

Jack Mapanje

Seasoned Jacarandas

(*for Frank Chipasula*)

Stiff collared, hands in pockets,
spitting out phlegm and scanning
the point of thankless patriotic
wakes and timid nights, we lied
brother, believing we would soon
arrive, someone must hang around,
knowing there would be no pieces
(the true warmth was outside). Today,
though seasoned, our metaphors
blanch. The jacarandas still deeply
purple our pavements; but for once
their pop under foot or tyre chills,
like those still fresh squads firing.
Who'll watch whose wake tomorrow,
this self-imposed siege trembles!

(*1993*)

Boraginaceae: Borage family

Amy Clampitt

Botanical Nomenclature

Down East people, not being botanists,
call it 'that pink-and-blue flower
you find along the shore.' Wildflower
guides, their minds elsewhere, mumble
'sea lungwort or oysterleaf' as a label
for these recumbent roundels, foliage
blued to a driftwood patina
growing outward, sometimes to the
size of a cathedral window,
stemrib grisaille edge-tasseled
with opening goblets, with bugles
in miniature, mauve through cerulean,
toggled into a seawall scree,
these tuffets of skyweed
neighbored by a climbing tideline,
by the holdfasts, the gargantuan lariats
of kelp, a landfall of seaweed:

Mertensia, the learned Latin
handle, proving the uses of taxonomy,
shifts everything abruptly inland,
childhoodward, to what we called then
(though not properly) bluebells:
spring-bottomland glades standing upright,
their lake-evoking sky color
a trapdoor, a window letting in distances
all the way to the ocean —
reaching out, *nolens volens*,
as one day everything breathing
will reach out, with just such
bells on its fingers, to touch
without yet quite having seen
the unlikelihood, the ramifying

happenstance, the mirroring
marryings of all likeness.

(*1984*)

Mertensia maritima
gromwell, sea lungwort, oysterleaf

Northern temperate coastlines

Christina Rossetti

A Bed of Forget-me-nots

Is love so prone to change and rot
We are fain to rear forget-me-not
By measure in a garden plot? —

I love its growth at large and free
By untrod path and unlopped tree,
Or nodding by the unpruned hedge,
Or on the water's dangerous edge
Where flags and meadowsweet blow rank
With rushes on the quaking bank.

Love is not taught in learning's school,
Love is not parcelled out by rule;
Hath curb or call an answer got? —
So free must be forget-me-not.
Give me the flame no dampness dulls,
The passion of the instinctive pulse,
Love steadfast as a fixèd star,
Tender as doves with nestlings are,
More large than time, more strong than death:
This all creation travails of —
She groans not for a passing breath —
This is forget-me-not and love.

(1856, *1896*)

Myosotis sylvatica
forget-me-not

Eurasia

Bromeliaceae: Bromeliad family

Hart Crane

The Air Plant

Grand Cayman

This tuft that thrives on saline nothingness,
Inverted octopus with heavenward arms
Thrust parching from a palm-bole hard by the cove —
A bird almost — of almost bird alarms,

Is pulmonary to the wind that jars
Its tentacles, horrific in their lurch.
The lizard's throat, held bloated for a fly,
Balloons but warily from this throbbing perch.

The needles and hack-saws of cactus bleed
A milk of earth when stricken off the stalk;
But this, — defenseless, thornless, sheds no blood,
Almost no shadow — but the air's thin talk.

Angelic Dynamo! Ventriloquist of the Blue!
While beachward creeps the shark-swept Spanish Main
By what conjunction do the winds appoint
Its apotheosis, at last — the hurricane!

(*1928*)

Tillandsia caput-medusae
air plant

Mexico

Cactaceae: Cactus family

Matthew Sweeney

Cacti

After she left he bought another cactus
just like the one she'd bought him
in the airport in Marrakesh. He had to hunt
through London, and then, in Camden,
among hordes of hand-holding kids
who clog the market, he found it,
bought it, and brought it home to hers.
Next week he was back for another,
then another. He was coaxed into trying
different breeds, bright ones flashing red —
like the smile of the shop-girl
he hadn't noticed. He bought a rug, too,
sand-coloured, for the living-room,
and spent a weekend repainting
the walls beige, the ceiling pale blue.
He had the worn, black suite re-upholstered
in tan, and took to lying on the sofa
in a brown djellaba, with the cacti all around,
and Arab music on. If she should come back,
he thought, she might feel at home.

(*1992*)

Cactaceae, Agavaceae spp.
cacti

North-west, especially hot and dry regions, Old-World tropics

James Wright

To the Saguaro Cactus Tree in the Desert Rain

I had no idea the elf owl
Crept into you in the secret
Of night.

I have torn myself out of many bitter places
In America, that seemed
Tall and green-rooted in mid-noon.
I wish I were the spare shadow
Of the roadrunner, I wish I were
The honest lover of the diamondback
And the tear the tarantula weeps.

I had no idea you were so tall
And blond in moonlight.

I got thirsty in the factories,
And I hated the brutal dry suns there,
So I quit.

You were the shadow
Of a hallway
In me.

I have never gone through that door,
But the elf owl's face
Is inside me.

Saguaro,
You are not one of the gods.

Your green arms lower and gather me.
I am an elf owl's shadow, a secret
Member of your family.

(*1977*)

Carnegiea gigantea
giant cactus

South-west United States, Mexico
The largest of all cacti, reaching 20m tall, 60cm thick, 12 tonnes in weight and alleged to live for 200 years

Robert Hayden

The Night-Blooming Cereus

  And so for nights
we waited, hoping to see
the heavy bud
  break into flower.

  On its neck-like tube
hooking down from the edge
of the leaf-branch
  nearly to the floor,

  the bud packed
tight with its miracle swayed
stiffly on breaths
  of air, moved

  as though impelled
by stirrings within itself.
It repelled as much
  as it fascinated me

  sometimes — snake,
eyeless bird head,
beak that would gape
  with grotesque life-squawk.

  But you, my dear,
conceded less to the bizarre
than to the imminence
  of bloom. Yet we agreed

  we ought
to celebrate the blossom,
paint ourselves, dance
  in honor of

  archaic mysteries
when it appeared. Meanwhile
we waited, aware
  of rigorous design.

Backster's
polygraph, I thought
would have shown
(as clear as it had

a philodendron's
fear) tribal sentience
in the cactus, focused
energy of will.

That belling of
tropic perfume — that
signaling
not meant for us;

the darkness
cloyed with summoning
fragrance. We dropped
trivial tasks

and marveling
beheld at last the achieved
flower. Its moonlight
petals were

still unfold-
ing, the spike fringe of the outer
perianth recessing
as we watched.

Luna presence,
foredoomed, already dying,
it charged the room
with plangency

older than human
cries, ancient as prayers
invoking Osiris, Krishna,
Tezcátlipóca.

We spoke
in whispers when
we spoke
at all . . .

(*1972*)

Selenicereus grandiflorus
night-blooming cereus

Cuba and Jamaica, naturalised throughout tropical America

Caprifoliaceae: Honeysuckle family

Don Paterson

Twinflooer

Tho' it grows
in oor baald east *bald*
alane, it's still *alone*
sic an antrin baste *rare beast*
I anely find it
in dwam or dream, *daydream*
an catch them
in thir lemanrie *sexual, illicit love*
hunkered alow
a wheesh't circle *stilled*
cut clean fae
the blackie-sang *blackbird*
or lintie-sang *linnet*
as ower a cairn,
or wirrikow *scarecrow or demon*
in a field o corn.

I part the girss *grass*
an' there they are,
the shilpit pair *thin*
cried for him *named*
wha rived a kingdom *split*
in twa estates, *two*
an' gently lift
the pallie, lither *pale, lazy*
bells thegither: *together*
twa fingertips
tak'in up
the exact wecht *weight*
o nothin, licht *light*
as the twa-fauld name
on yer ane jimp stem. *slender*

Win'-balance,
elf-cleek, *hook*
breist o silence — *breast*
a word hauf-swicked *cheated*
fae the fa' o Babel,
whitever it spelt
sae slicht and nesh *slight, soft*
it jinked the trouble, *dodged*
and rode the jaw *wave*
as the broch tummel't — *tower*
t' somehow waash
up here, a trick
or holy geg *gag*
like the *twa-in-yin* *'horseman's word'*
breathed in the lug *ear*
o the blin'fauld halflin. *adolescent*

Ma jo, they say *dear or sweetheart*
oor nation's nae
words for *love*
the wiy we have
for daith or deil. *death, devil*
Times ye feel
the mair wi gang *more, go*
intil thon tongue —
hidden, fey *doomed*
an' ayebydan — *eternal*
the less wi hae
the need o ane.

And jist the same
there's nae flooer here
aside the yin
I've here descreivit. *described*
Yet merk this pair,
strecht fae Ovid, *straight*
nailed thegither
wame to wame; *belly*
tynt in the ither, *lost*
ayont a' thocht, *beyond, thought*
a' deed, a' talk,
hauf-jyned, hauf-rift — *joined*

thir heids doverin *nodding in sleep*
unner the licht
  yock *yoke*
o the lift *sky*

(*2001*)

Linnaea borealis
twinflower

Circumpolar regions, including Europe

Caryophyllaceae: Pink family

Theodore Roethke

Carnations

Pale blossoms, each balanced on a single jointed stem,
The leaves curled back in elaborate Corinthian scrolls;
And the air cool, as if drifting down from wet hemlocks,
Or rising out of ferns not far from water,
A crisp hyacinthine coolness,
Like that clear autumnal weather of eternity,
The windless perpetual morning above a September cloud.

(*1948*)

Dianthus caryophyllus
carnation

Mediterranean

Casuarinaceae: Casuarina family

Toru Dutt

Our Casuarina Tree

Like a huge Python, winding round and round
  The rugged trunk, indented deep with scars
  Up to its very summit near the stars,
A creeper climbs, in whose embraces bound
  No other tree could live. But gallantly
The giant wears the scarf, and flowers are hung
In crimson clusters all the boughs among,
  Whereon all day are gathered bird and bee;
And oft at nights the garden overflows
With one sweet song that seems to have no close,
Sung darkling from our tree, while men repose.

When first my casement is wide open thrown
  At dawn, my eyes delighted on it rest;
  Sometimes, and most in winter, — on its crest
A gray baboon sits statue-like alone
  Watching the sunrise; while on lower boughs
His puny offspring leap about and play;
And far and near kokilas hail the day;
  And to their pastures wend our sleepy cows;
And in the shadow, on the broad tank cast
By that hoar tree, so beautiful and vast,
The water-lilies spring, like snow enmassed.

But not because of its magnificence
  Dear is the Casuarina to my soul:
  Beneath it we have played; though years may roll,
O sweet companions, loved with love intense,
  For your sakes shall the tree be ever dear!
Blent with your images, it shall arise
In memory, till the hot tears blind mine eyes!
  What is that dirge-like murmur that I hear
Like the sea breaking on a shingle-beach?

It is the tree's lament, an eerie speech,
That haply to the unknown land may reach.

Unknown, yet well-known to the eye of faith!
  Ah, I have heard that wail far, far away
  In distant lands, by many a sheltered bay,
When slumbered in his cave the water-wraith
  And the waves gently kissed the classic shore
Of France or Italy, beneath the moon,
When earth lay trancèd in a dreamless swoon:
  And every time the music rose, — before
Mine inner vision rose a form sublime,
Thy form, O Tree, as in my happy prime
I saw thee, in my own loved native clime.

Therefore I fain would consecrate a lay
  Unto thy honour, Tree, beloved of those
  Who now in blessed sleep, for aye, repose,
Dearer than life to me, alas! were they!
  Mayst thou be numbered when my days are done
With deathless trees — like those in Borrowdale,
Under whose awful branches lingered pale
  'Fear, trembling Hope, and Death, the skeleton,
And Time the shadow'; and though weak the verse
That would thy beauty fain, oh fain rehearse,
May Love defend thee from Oblivion's curse.

(*1882*)

Casuarina equisetifolia
Australian pine, beefwood, jau, whistling pine, yar

Indo-Malaysia

Roland Robinson

Casuarina

The last, the long-haired casuarina
stands upon the hillside where
against the turquoise night of those first
yellow stars, she shakes her hair.

She shakes her hair out in her singing
of cliffs and caves and waterfalls,
and tribes who left the lichened sandstone
carved in gods and animals.

This is her country: honeyeaters
cry out its Aboriginal name
where on her ridges still the spear tall
lilies burn in flame and flame.

I listen, and our legend says not
more than this dark singing tree,
although her golden flowering lover
lies slain beside the winter sea.

(*1989*)

Casuarina cunninghamiana
river oak

Eastern Australia

Colchicaceae: Autumn Crocus family

Ruth Fainlight

Autumn Crocus

Anomalous bright blossom
in late afternoon shadow.

Mercury-pale stems
surging out of the dark
earth: Halloween candles.

Mauve flowers with amber
yellow pollen-swollen anthers.

Each clump is bordered
by a halo of rotting
petals like votive objects
around a damaged ikon
or a martyr's statue.

(*1997*)

Colchicum autumnale
meadow saffron, naked boys

Europe to North Africa

Combretaceae: Sea-Almond family

Derek Walcott

The Almond Trees

There's nothing here
this early;
cold sand
cold churning ocean, the Atlantic,
no visible history,

except this stand
of twisted, coppery, sea-almond trees
their shining postures surely
bent as metal, and one

foam-haired, salt-grizzled fisherman,
his mongrel growling, whirling on the stick
he pitches him; its spinning rays
'no visible history'
until their lengthened shapes amaze the sun.

By noon,
this further shore of Africa is strewn
with the forked limbs of girls toasting their flesh
in scarves, sunglasses, Pompeian bikinis,

brown daphnes, laurels, they'll all have
like their originals, their sacred grove,
this frieze
of twisted, coppery, sea-almond trees.

The fierce acetylene air
has singed
their writhing trunks with rust, the same
hues as a foundered, peeling barge.
It'll sear a pale skin copper with its flame.

The sand's white-hot ash underheel,
but their aged limbs have got their brazen sheen

from fire. Their bodies fiercely shine!
They're cured,
they endured their furnace.

Aged trees and oiled limbs share a common colour!

Welded in one flame,
huddling naked, stripped of their name,
for Greek or Roman tags, they were lashed
raw by wind, washed
out with salt and fire-dried,
bitterly nourished where their branches died,

their leaves' broad dialect a coarse,
enduring sound
they shared together.

Not as some running hamadryad's cries
rooted, broke slowly into leaf
her nipples peaking to smooth, wooden boles.

Their grief
howls seaward through charred, ravaged holes.

One sunburnt body now acknowledges
that past and its own metamorphosis
as, moving from the sun, she kneels to spread
her wrap within the bent arms of this grove
that grieves in silence, like parental love.

(*1965*)

Terminalia catappa
Indian, Barbados or wild almond

Indo-Malaysia

Compositae: Daisy family

John Clare

The Yarrow

Dweller in pastoral spots, life gladly learns
That nature never mars her aim to please;
Thy dark leaves, like to clumps of little ferns,
Imbue my walk with feelings such as these;
O'ertopt with swarms of flowers that charms the sight,
Some blushing into pink and others white,
On meadow banks, roadsides, and on the leas
Of rough, neglected pastures, I delight
More even than in gardens thus to stray
Amid such scenes and mark thy hardy blooms
Peering into the autumn's mellowing day;
The mower's scythe swept summer blooms away
Where thou, defying dreariness, wilt come
Bidding the loneliest russet paths be gay.

(1832–5, *1935*)

Achillea millefolium
milfoil

Europe, west Asia, widely naturalised in temperate regions

Edward Thomas

Old Man

Old Man, or Lad's-love, — in the name there's nothing
To one that knows not Lad's-love, or Old Man,
The hoar-green feathery herb, almost a tree,
Growing with rosemary and lavender.
Even to one that knows it well, the names
Half decorate, half perplex, the thing it is:
At least, what that is clings not to the names
In spite of time. And yet I like the names.

The herb itself I like not, but for certain
I love it, as some day the child will love it
Who plucks a feather from the door-side bush
Whenever she goes in or out of the house.
Often she waits there, snipping the tips and shrivelling
The shreds at last on to the path, perhaps
Thinking, perhaps of nothing, till she sniffs
Her fingers and runs off. The bush is still
But half as tall as she, though it is as old;
So well she clips it. Not a word she says;
And I can only wonder how much hereafter
She will remember, with that bitter scent,
Of garden rows, and ancient damson trees
Topping a hedge, a bent path to a door,
A low thick bush beside the door, and me
Forbidding her to pick.
As for myself,
Where first I met the bitter scent is lost.
I, too, often shrivel the grey shreds,
Sniff them and think and sniff again and try
Once more to think what it is I am remembering,
Always in vain. I cannot like the scent,
Yet I would rather give up others more sweet,
With no meaning, than this bitter one.
I have mislaid the key. I sniff the spray
And think of nothing; I see and I hear nothing;
Yet seem, too, to be listening, lying in wait
For what I should, yet never can, remember:
No garden appears, no path, no hoar-green bush

Of Lad's-love, or Old Man, no child beside,
Neither father nor mother, nor any playmate;
Only an avenue, dark, nameless, without end.

(*1917*)

Artemisia abrotanum
southernwood, lad's love, old man

Probably southern Europe (origin unknown)

Robert Burns

To a Mountain-Daisy

On turning one down, with the Plough, in April 1786

Wee, modest, crimson-tipped flow'r,
Thou's met me in an evil hour;
For I maun crush amang the stoure
They slender stem:
To spare thee now is past my pow'r,
Thou bonie gem.

Alas! it's no thy neebor sweet,
The bonie *Lark*, companion meet!
Bending thee 'mang the dewy weet!
Wi's spreckl'd breast,
When upward-springing, blythe, to greet
The purpling East.

Cauld blew the bitter-biting *North*
Upon thy early, humble birth;
Yet chearfully thou glinted forth
Amid the storm,
Scarce rear'd above the *Parent-earth*
Thy tender form.

The flaunting *flow'rs* our Gardens yield,
High-shelt'ring woods and wa's maun shield,
But thou, beneath the random bield
O' clod or stane,
Adorns the histie *stibble-field*,
Unseen, alane.

There, in thy scanty mantle clad,
Thy snawie bosom sun-ward spread,
Thou lifts thy unassuming head
In humble guise;
But now the *share* uptears thy bed,
And low thou lies!

Such is the fate of artless Maid,
Sweet *flow'ret* of the rural shade!
By Love's simplicity betray'd,
And guileless trust,

Till she, like thee, all soil'd, is laid
Low i' the dust.

Such is the fate of simple Bard,
On Life's rough ocean luckless starr'd!
Unskilful he to note the card
Of *prudent Lore*,
Till billows rage, and gales blow hard,
And whelm him o'er!

Such fate to *suffering worth* is giv'n,
Who long with wants and woes has striv'n,
By human pride or cunning driv'n
To Mis'ry's brink,
Till wrench'd of ev'ry stay but Heav'n,
He, ruin'd, sink!

Ev'n thou who mourn'st the *Daisy's* fate,
That fate is thine — no distant date;
Stern Ruin's *plough-share* drives, elate,
Full on thy bloom,
Till crush'd beneath the *furrow's* weight,
Shall be thy doom!

(*1786*)

Bellis perennis
daisy

Mediterranean

John Clare

The Daisy

The daisy is a happy flower,
  And comes at early spring,
And brings with it the sunny hour
  When bees are on the wing.

It brings with it the butterfly,
  And early humble-bee;
With the polyanthus' golden eye,
  And blooming apple-tree;

Hedge-sparrows from the mossy nest
  In the old garden hedge,
Where schoolboys, in their idle glee,
  Seek pooties as their pledge.

The cow stands browsing all the day
  Over the orchard gate,
And eats her bit of sweet old hay;
  And Goody stands to wait,

Lest what's not eaten the rude wind
  May rise and snatch away
Over the neighbour's hedge behind,
  Where hungry cattle lay.

(10 February 1860, *1935*)

Robert Herrick

To Daisies, *Not to Shut So Soone*

1. Shut not so soon; the dull-ey'd night
   Ha's not as yet begunne
   To make a seisure on the light,
   Or to seale up the Sun.

2. No Marigolds yet closed are;
   No shadowes great appeare;
   Nor doth the early Shepheards Starre
   Shine like a spangle here.

3. Stay but till my *Julia* close
   Her life-begetting eye;
   And let the whole world then dispose
   It selfe to live or dye.

(*1648*)

daisy = day's eye, because the flower closes at night

George Wither

The Marigold

Whilst I, the Sunne's *bright Face may view,*
I will no meaner Light *pursue.*

When, with a serious musing, I behold
The gratefull, and obsequious *Marigold*,
How duely, ev'ry morning, she displayes
Her open brest, when *Titan* spreads his Rayes;
How she observes him in his daily walke,
Still bending towards him, her tender stalke;
How, when he downe declines, she droopes and mournes,
Bedew'd (as t'were) with teares, till he returnes;
And, how she vailes her *Flow'rs*, when he is gone,
As if she scorned to be looked on
By an inferior *Eye*; or, did contemne
To wayt upon a meaner *Light*, then *Him*.
When this I meditate, me-thinkes, the *Flowers*
Have *Spirits*, farre more generous, then ours;
And, give us faire Examples, to despise
The servile Fawnings, and Idolatries,
Wherewith, we court these earthly things below,
Which merit not the service we bestow.
  But, oh my God! though groveling I appeare
Upon the Ground, (and have a rooting here,
Which hales me downward) yet in my desire,
To that, which is above mee, I aspire:
And, all my best *Affections* I professe
To *Him*, that is the *Sunne of Righteousnesse*.
Oh! keepe the *Morning* of his *Incarnation*,
The burning *Noon-tide* of his bitter *Passion*,
The *Night* of his *Descending*, and the *Height*

Of his *Ascension*, ever in my sight:
  That imitating him, in what I may,
  I never follow an inferior *Way*.

(*1634*)

Calendula officinalis
common, pot or Scotch marigold, ruddles

Origin unclear

Vicki Feaver

Marigolds

Not the flowers men give women —
delicately-scented freesias,
stiff red roses, carnations
the shades of bridesmaids' dresses,
almost sapless flowers,
drying and fading — but flowers
that wilt as soon as their stems
are cut, leaves blackening
as if blighted by the enzymes
in our breath, rotting to a slime
we have to scour from the rims
of vases; flowers that burst
from tight, explosive buds, rayed
like the sun, that lit the path
up the Thracian mountain, that we wound
into our hair, stamped on
in ecstatic dance, that remind us
we are killers, can tear the heads
off men's shoulders;
flowers we still bring
secretly and shamefully
into the house, stroking
our arms and breasts and legs
with their hot orange fringes,
the smell of arousal.

(*1994*)

John Clare

The Fear of Flowers

The nodding oxeye bends before the wind,
The woodbine quakes lest boys their flowers should find,
And prickly dog rose, spite of its array
Can't dare the blossom-seeking hand away,
While thistles wear their heavy knobs of bloom
Proud as a war horse wears its haughty plume,
And by the roadside danger's self defies;
On commons where pined sheep and oxen lie
In ruddy pomp and ever thronging mood
It stands and spreads like danger in a wood,
And in the village street where meanest weeds
Can't stand untouched to fill their husks with seed,
The haughty thistle o'er all danger towers,
In every place the very wasp of flowers.

(1824–32, *1908*)

Cirsium vulgare
spear thistle, bull thistle

Europe and the Mediterranean, naturalised in North America

Ted Hughes

Thistles

Against the rubber tongues of cows and the hoeing hands of
  men
Thistles spike the summer air
Or crackle open under a blue-black pressure.

Every one a revengeful burst
Of resurrection, a grasped fistful
Of splintered weapons and Icelandic frost thrust up

From the underground stain of a decayed Viking.
They are like pale hair and the gutturals of dialects.
Every one manages a plume of blood.

Then they grow grey, like men.
Mown down, it is a feud. Their sons appear,
Stiff with weapons, fighting back over the same ground.

(*1967*)

Rita Dove

Then Came Flowers

I should have known if you gave me flowers
They would be chrysanthemums.
The white spikes singed my fingers.
I cried out; they spilled from the green tissue
And spread at my feet in a pool of soft fire.

If I begged you to stay, what good would it do me?
In the bed, you would lay the flowers between us.
I will pick them up later, arrange them with pincers.
All night from the bureau they'll watch me, their
Plumage as proud, as cocky as firecrackers.

(*1980*)

Dendranthema spp.
chrysanthemums

East Asia
Probably a complex hybrid group raised in China, with 500 cultivars by 1630; introduced to Europe 1688, established in France 1789

‘Robin Hyde’ (Iris Guiver Wilkinson)

Chrysanthemum

See that dishevelled head,
Its bronze curls all undone?
I am that one,
The stubborn slattern of your garden bed;
No sweetness for you here, but bittersweet
Admission that my hour must needs be fleet;
A frosty tang of wit, an autumn face,
Perchance the memory of some sharper grace,
That shone beneath the imperial yellow tiles
Nor needed stoop for princely sulks or smiles;
Tatterdemalion courage here, a ghost
To captain some obscure, defeated host . . .
Many the springtime maidens, crisp as snow . . .
Yet, hapless sir, we know
Your fate . . . to love me most.

(*1937*)

William Blake

Ah! Sun-flower

Ah Sun-flower! weary of time,
Who countest the steps of the Sun:
Seeking after that sweet golden clime,
Where the traveller's journey is done.

Where the Youth pined away with desire,
And the pale Virgin shrouded in snow:
Arise from their graves and aspire,
Where my Sun-flower wishes to go.

(*1794*)

Helianthus annuus
sunflower

North America; introduced to Europe in 1510

Allen Ginsberg

Sunflower Sutra

I walked on the banks of the tincan banana dock and sat down under the huge shade of a Southern Pacific locomotive to look at the sunset over the box house hills and cry.
Jack Kerouac sat beside me on a busted rusty iron pole, companion, we thought the same thoughts of the soul, bleak and blue and sad-eyed, surrounded by the gnarled steel roots of trees of machinery.
The oily water on the river mirrored the red sky, sun sank on top of final Frisco peaks, no fish in that stream, no hermit in those mounts, just ourselves rheumy-eyed and hung-over like old bums on the riverbank, tired and wily.
Look at the Sunflower, he said, there was a dead gray shadow against the sky, big as a man, sitting dry on top of a pile of ancient sawdust —
— I rushed up enchanted — it was my first sunflower, memories of Blake — my visions — Harlem
and Hells of the Eastern rivers, bridges clanking Joes Greasy Sandwiches, dead baby carriages, black treadless tires forgotten and unretreaded, the poem of the riverbank, condoms & pots, steel knives, nothing stainless, only the dank muck and the razor-sharp artifacts passing into the past —
and the gray Sunflower poised against the sunset, crackly bleak and dusty with the smut and smog and smoke of olden locomotives in its eye —
corolla of bleary spikes pushed down and broken like a battered crown, seeds fallen out of its face, soon-to-be-toothless mouth of sunny air, sunrays obliterated on its hairy head like a dried wire spider-web,
leaves stuck out like arms out of the stem, gestures from the sawdust root, broke pieces of plaster fallen out of the black twigs, a dead fly in its ear,
Unholy battered old thing you were, my sunflower O my soul, I loved you then!
The grime was no man's grime but death and human locomotives,
all that dress of dust, that veil of darkened railroad skin, that smog of cheek, that eyelid of black mis'ry, that sooty hand or phallus or protuberance of artificial worse-than-dirt —

industrial — modern — all that civilization spotting your crazy
golden crown —
and those blear thoughts of death and dusty loveless eyes and
ends and withered roots below, in the home-pile of sand and
sawdust, rubber dollar bills, skin of machinery, the guts and
innards of the weeping coughing car, the empty lonely tincans
with their rusty tongues alack, what more could I name, the
smoked ashes of some cock cigar, the cunts of wheelbarrows
and the milky breasts of cars, wornout asses out of chairs &
sphincters of dynamos — all these
entangled in your mummied roots — and you there standing
before me in the sunset, all your glory in your form!
A perfect beauty of a sunflower! a perfect excellent lovely
sunflower existence! a sweet natural eye to the new hip moon,
woke up alive and excited grasping in the sunset shadow
sunrise golden monthly breeze!
How many flies buzzed round you innocent of your grime,
while you cursed the heavens of the railroad and your flower
soul?
Poor dead flower? when did you forget you were a flower? when
did you look at your skin and decide you were an impotent
dirty old locomotive? the ghost of a locomotive? the specter
and shade of a once powerful mad American locomotive?
You were never no locomotive, Sunflower, you were a sunflower!
And you Locomotive, you are a locomotive, forget me not!
So I grabbed up the skeleton thick sunflower and stuck it at my
side like a scepter,
and deliver my sermon to my soul, and Jack's soul too, and
anyone who'll listen,
— We're not our skin of grime, we're not dread bleak dusty
imageless locomotives, we're golden sunflowers inside, blessed
by our own seed & hairy naked accomplishment-bodies
growing into mad black formal sunflowers in the sunset, spied
on by our own eyes under the shadow of the mad locomotive
riverbank sunset Frisco hilly tincan evening sitdown vision.

BERKELEY

(*1955*)

Jamie McKendrick

Chrome Yellow

Your three brave sunflowers are ready to drop.
Standing in a jug of stale drink
they've all about reached a steepening patch
on the curve of decay. Their dark-eyed
flameheads raddle at the tips and close
then, lax as pulp or crape, they start to droop
on thick eyestalks. That mad Dutchman
who crammed his mouth with the chrome yellow
he used by the tubeful to paint them
made toxic lead his edible gold.
Their gold now lead, the sunflowers turn
towards the black sun of the earth.
Their time has gone. Their big leaves drape
and darken round them like a field of crows.

(*2001*)

John Clare

The Ragwort

Ragwort, thou humble flower with tattered leaves,
I love to see thee come and litter gold,
What time the summer binds her russet sheaves;
Decking rude spots in beauties manifold,
That without thee were dreary to behold,
Sunburnt and bare — the meadow bank, the baulk
That leads a wagon-way through mellow fields,
Rich with the tints that harvest's plenty yields,
Browns of all hues; and everywhere I walk
Thy waste of shining blossoms richly shields
The sunburnt sward, in splendid hues, that burn
So bright and glaring that the very light
Of the rich sunshine doth to paleness turn,
And seems but very shadows in thy sight.

(1832–5, *1924*)

Senecio jacobaea
ragwort

Europe and the Mediterranean

Howard Nemerov

Dandelions

These golden heads, these common suns
Only less multitudinous
Than grass itself that gluts
The market of the world with green,
They shine as lovely as they're mean,
Fine as the daughters of the poor
Who go proudly in spangles of brass;
Light-headed, then headless, stalked for a salad.

Inside a week they will be seen
Stricken and old, ghosts in the field
To be picked up at the lightest breath,
With brazen tops all shrunken in
And swollen green gone withered white.
You'll say it's nature's price for beauty
That goes cheap; that being light
Is justly what makes girls grow heavy;
And that the wind, bearing their death,
Whispers the second kingdom come.
— You'll say, the fool of piety,
By resignations hanging on
Until, still justified, you drop.
But surely the thing is sorrowful,
At evening, when the light goes out
Slowly, to see those ruined spinsters,
All down the field their ghostly hair,
Dry sinners waiting in the valley
For the last word and the next life
And the liberation from the lion's mouth.

(*1955*)

Taraxacum officinale
dandelion

Eurasia

May Swenson

Little Lion Face

Little lion face
I stooped to pick
among the mass of thick
succulent blooms, the twice

streaked flanges of your silk
sunwheel relaxed in wide
dilation, I brought inside,
placed in a vase. Milk

of your shaggy stem
sticky on my fingers, and
your barbs hooked to my hand,
sudden stings from them

were sweet. Now I'm bold
to touch your swollen neck,
put careful lips to slick
petals, snuff up gold

pollen in your navel cup.
Still fresh before night
I leave you, dawn's appetite
to renew our glide and suck.

An hour ahead of sun
I come to find you. You're
twisted shut as a burr,
neck drooped unconscious,

an inert, limp bundle,
a furled cocoon, your
sun-streaked aureole
eclipsed and dun.

Strange feral flower asleep
with flame-ruff wilted,
all magic halted,
a drink I pour, steep

in the glass for your
undulant stem to suck.

Oh, lift your young neck,
open and expand to your

lover, hot light.
Gold corona, widen to sky.
I hold you lion in my eye
sunup until night.

(*1987*)

Janet Sylvester

Goatsbeard

In light limpid as standing snowmelt
and as palely green, the season's first
globular goatsbeard arranges the roadside cut.
Its weightless seeds commute to distances
on the wind's thick taproot, everywhere.

How can you look at me as you do,
as if I were that common herb?
My body breaks within your gaze, milky,
into what you want to disappear.

The mind, a delicate fiber at the top
of each occasion, allows me
to escape. This parachute, how can I tell,
means that you seed all over the place,
yellow salsify, related species.

Yours, mine, the goatsbeard appears
suspended, singular in late, late sun.
Inside it are a thousand mirrors
and, inside us, your need for one.

In fact, it has no form at all.
I look at it and say its name,
Tragopogon dubius, to you in this way
as you say *Janet*, the trade name
Our purposes are elsewhere certified.

Yes, this potent early evening takes us
to itself as if the code could be undone.
We're trained so, to be happy standing
in the tree's shadow, thinking,

what's happening now? A half-bird catches
in the eye, a fluid slash of black,
a plea: Come back, come back,
we need to promote each other
as that sibilance hissing into speed,

deepening blue's oldest promotion
over shapes, defines shaped sides.

What grows wild is doubly beautiful.
What grows wild is a disguise.

Not badly formed. Take my hand,
being impervious to meaning in its bones
carefully snapping the goatsbeard from near grasses,
as the goatsbeard comes apart here
and there, its life dissembling.

Somewhere a set of premises keeps us
apart. Whomever I was talking to
through this day's economy of green
holds in space between the eye and mind
a thousand, shining girders.

(*1997*)

Tragopogon pratensis
goatsbeard

Europe, naturalised in North America

Convallariaceae: Lily-of-the-Valley

Ezra Pound

Alba

As cool as the pale wet leaves
                    of lily-of-the-valley
She lay beside me in the dawn.

(*1913*)

Convallaria majalis
lily-of-the-valley

Europe

Convolvulaceae: Bindweed family

Louise Glück

Ipomoea

What was my crime in another life,
as in this life my crime
is sorrow, that I am not to be
permitted to ascend ever again,
never in any sense
permitted to repeat my life,
wound in the hawthorn, all
earthly beauty my punishment
as it is yours —
Source of my suffering, why
have you drawn from me
these flowers like the sky, except
to mark me as a part
of my master: I am
his cloak's color, my flesh giveth
form to his glory.

(*1992*)

Ipomoea tricolor
morning glory

Mexico and Central America

Ruth Pitter

Morning Glory

With a pure colour there is little one can do:
Of a pure thing there is little one can say.
We are dumb in the face of that cold blush of blue,
Called glory, and enigmatic as the face of day.

A couple of optical tricks are there for the mind;
See how the azure darkens as we recede:
Like the delectable mountains left behind,
Region and colour too absolute for our need.

Or putting an eye too close, until it blurs,
You see a firmament, a ring of sky,
With a white radiance in it, a universe,
And something there that might seem to sing and fly.

Only the double sex, the usual thing;
But it calls to mind spirit, it seems like the one
Who hovers in brightness suspended and shimmering,
Crying Holy and hanging in the eye of the sun.

And there is one thing more; as in despair
The eye dwells on that ribbed pentagonal round,
A cold sidereal whisper brushes the ear,
A prescient tingling, a prophecy of sound.

(*1966*)

Cupressaceae: Cypress family

Aphra Behn

On a Juniper-Tree Cut Down to Make Busks

Whilst happy I Triumphant stood,
The Pride and Glory of the Wood;
My Aromatick Boughs and Fruit,
Did with all other Trees dispute.
Had right by Nature to excel,
In pleasing both the tast and smell:
But to the touch I must confess,
Bore an ungrateful Sullenness.
My Wealth, like bashful Virgins, I
Yielded with some Reluctancy;
For which my vallue should be more,
Not giving easily my store.
My verdant Branches all the year
Did an Eternal Beauty wear;
Did ever young and gay appear.
Nor needed any tribute pay,
For bounties from the God of Day:
Nor do I hold Supremacy,
(In all the Wood) o'er every Tree.
But even those too of my own Race,
That grow not in this happy place.
But that in which I glory most,
And do my self with Reason boast,
Beneath my shade the other day,
Young *Philocles* and *Cloris* lay,
Upon my Root she lean'd her head,
And where I grew, he made their Bed:
Whilst I the Canopy more largely spread.
Their trembling Limbs did gently press,
The kind supporting yielding Grass:
Ne'er half so blest as now, to bear
A Swain so Young, a Nimph so fair:
My Grateful Shade I kindly lent,

And every aiding Bough I bent.
So low, as sometimes had the blisse,
To rob the Shepherd of a kiss,
Whilst he in Pleasures far above
The Sence of tht degree of Love:
Permitted every stealth I made,
Unjealous of his Rival Shade.
I saw 'em kindle to desire,
Whilst with soft sighs they blew the fire:
Saw the approaches of their joy,
He growing more fierce, and she less Coy,
Saw how they mingled melting Rays,
Exchanging Love a thousand ways.
Kind was the force on every side,
Her new desire she could not hide:
Nor wou'd the Shepherd be deny'd.
Impatient he waits no consent
But what she gave by Languishment,
The blessed Minute he pursu'd;
And now transported in his Arms,
Yeilds to the Conqueror all her Charmes,
His panting Breast, to hers now join'd,
They feast on Raptures unconfin'd;
Vast and Luxuriant, such as prove
The Immortality of Love.
For who but a Divinitie,
Could mingle Souls to that Degree;
And melt 'em into Extasie.
Now like the *Phenix*, both Expire,
While from the Ashes of their fire,
Sprung up a new, and soft desire.
Like Charmers, thrice they did invoke,
The God! and thrice new vigor took.
Nor had the Mysterie ended there,
But *Cloris* reassum'd her fear,
And chid the Swain, for having prest,
What she alas wou'd not resist:
Whilst he in whom Loves sacred flame,
Before and after was the same,
Fondly implor'd she wou'd forget
A fault, which he wou'd yet repeat.

From Active Joyes with some they hast,
To a Reflexion on the past;
A thousand times my Covert bless,
That did secure their Happiness:
Their Gratitude to every Tree
They pay, but most to happy me;
The Shepherdess my Bark carest,
Whilst he my Root, Love's Pillow, kist;
And did with sighs, their Fate deplore,
Since I must shelter them no more;
And if before my Joyes were such,
In having heard, and seen too much,
My Grief must be as great and high,
When all abandon'd I shall be,
Doom'd to a silent Destinie.
No more the Charming strife to hear,
The Shepherds Vows, the Virgins fear:
No more a joyful looker on,
Whilst Loves soft Battel's lost and won.
With grief I bow'd my murmering Head,
And all my Christal Dew I shed.
Which did in *Cloris* Pity move,
(*Cloris* whose Soul is made of Love;)
She cut me down, and did translate,
My being to a happier state.
No Martyr for Religion di'd
With half that Unconsidering Pride;
My top was on that Altar laid,
Where Love his softest Offerings paid:
And was as fragrant Incense burn'd,
My body into Busks was turn'd:
Where I still guard the Sacred Store,
And of Loves Temple keep the Door.

(*1684*)

Juniperus communis
juniper

Northern temperate regions

Tom Paulin

from *The Book of Juniper*

Tougher than the wind
it keeps a low profile
on rough ground.
Rugged, fecund,
with resined spines,
the gymnosperm
hugs the hillside
and wills its own survival.
The subtle arts are still to happen
and in the eye of a needle
a singing voice
tells a miniature epic
of the boreal forest:
not a silk tapestry
of fierce folk
warring on the tundra
or making exquisite love
on a starry counterpane,
but an in-the-beginning
was a wintry light
and *juniperus*

*

On a bruised coast
I crush a blue bead
between my fingers,
tracing the scent, somewhere,
of that warm, mnemonic haybox,
burnished fields, a linen picnic
and a summer dawn
where mushrooms raise their domed gills.
They are white in the dew
and this nordic grape
whets an eager moment
of bodies meeting in a fishy fume.
Its meek astringency is distilled
into perfume and medicines,
it matches venison

as the sour gooseberry
cuts the oily mackerel.
Spicy, glaucous,
its branches fan out
like the wind's shadow
on long grass,
then melt back
and go to ground
where swart choughs
open their red beaks,
stinging the air
with stony voices.

*

Though it might be a simple
decoration
or a chill fragrance
in a snug souterrain,
I must grasp again
how its green
springy resistance
ducks its head down and skirts
the warped polities of other trees
bent in the Atlantic wind.
For no one knows
if nature allowed it
to grow tall
what proud grace
the juniper tree might show
that flared, once, like fire
along the hills.

*

On this coast
it is the only
tree of freedom
to be found,
and I imagine
that a swelling army is marching
from Memory Harbour and Killala

carrying branches
of green juniper.

Consider
the gothic zigzags
and brisk formations
that square to meet
the green tide rising
through Mayo and Antrim,

now dream
of that sweet
equal republic
where the juniper
talks to the oak,
the thistle,
the bandaged elm,
and the jolly jolly chestnut.

(*1984*)

Cycadaceae: Cycad family

Judith Wright

The Cycads

Their smooth dark flames flicker at time's own root.
Round them the rising forests of the years
alter the climates of forgotten earth
and silt with leaves the strata of first birth.

Only the antique cycads sullenly
keep the old bargain life has long since broken;
and, cursed by age, through each chill century
they watch the shrunken moon, but never die

for time forgets the promise he once made,
and change forgets that they are left alone.
Among the complicated birds and flowers
they seem a generation carved in stone.

Leaning together, down those gulfs they stare
over whose darkness dance the brilliant birds
that cry in air one moment, and are gone;
and with their countless suns the years spin on.

Take their cold seed and set it in the mind,
and its slow root will lengthen deep by deep
till, following, you cling on the last ledge
over the unthinkable, unfathomed edge
beyond which man remembers only sleep.

(*1949*)

Cycadaceae
Plants known as cycads include the families Boweniaceae, Stangeriaceae and Zamiaceae

Dracaenaceae: Dragon-Tree family

Ruth Dallas

Living with a Cabbage-tree

A cabbage-palm is not an interesting tree.
Its single trunk resembles a telegraph-pole.
Botanists say it is not a tree at all,
But a lily, grown exceptionally rampant.
This, I think, could happen only in New Zealand,
Where birds have left us skeletons as big as horses'.

I did not want a cabbage-tree in the garden.
There's plenty of room on the Canterbury plains
Where a tree of any kind relieves the eye.
Its life began as a little harmless flax-bush,
I thought a pot-plant — ornamental leaves
Someone had planted out for variety of foliage.
I had hardly turned my back when it soared up
Into a shape like a coconut-palm in a strait-jacket.

The flax-bush part is elevated now, say fifteen feet,
And casts the smallest patch of shadow and the fastest
In the garden. It's enough to cover your head;
But if you take a chair outside you must be prepared
To shift from west to east more quickly
Than you have ever chased the shelter of a tree.

I like the way the shadow of its bole
Moves like the finger of a giant sun-dial
Over the concrete; that's rather romantic;
Reminding us that time is passing, passing;
And cats declare it without peer for sharpening claws.
But it's a dull tree, inclined to fancy itself
As a musical instrument, when the wind blows,

Sometimes tuning up like an orchestra.
You listen expectantly. But nothing happens.
The wind drops and it falls silent.

(*1976*)

Cordyline australis
cabbage-tree

New Zealand

Droseraceae: Sundew family

Algernon Charles Swinburne

The Sundew

A little marsh-plant, yellow green,
And pricked at lip with tender red.
Tread close, and either way you tread
Some faint black water jets between
Lest you should bruise the curious head.

A live thing maybe; who shall know?
The summer knows and suffers it;
For the cool moss is thick and sweet
Each side, and saves the blossom so
That it lives out the long June heat.

The deep scent of the heather burns
About it; breathless though it be,
Bow down and worship; more than we
Is the least flower whose life returns,
Least weed renascent in the sea.

We are vexed and cumbered in earth's sight
With wants, with many memories;
These see their mother what she is,
Glad-growing, till August leave more bright
The apple-coloured cranberries.

Wind blows and bleaches the strong grass,
Blown all one way to shelter it
From temple of strayed kine, with feet
Felt heavier than the moorhen was,
Strayed up past patches of wild wheat.

You call it sundew: how it grows,
If with its colour it have breath,
If life taste sweet to it, if death
Pain its soft petal, no man knows:
Man has no sight or sense that saith.

My sundew, grown of gentle days,
In these green miles the spring begun
Thy growth ere April had half done
With the soft secret of her ways
Or June made ready for the sun.

O red-lipped mouth of marsh-flower,
I have a secret halved with thee.
The name that is love's name to me
Thou knowest, and the face of her
Who is my festival to see.

The hard sun, as thy petals knew,
Coloured the heavy moss-water:
Thou wert not worth green midsummer
Nor fit to live to August blue,
O sundew, not remembering her.

(*1866*)

Drosera anglica
sundew

Northern temperate regions

Norman MacCaig

Venus fly-trap

Ridding my mind of cant
With one deft twist of my most deep convictions,
I find you are less animal than plant.

You suck the rank soil in
And flourish, on your native commonplaces,
The lively signal of a sense of sin.

I buzzed and landed, but,
Encroaching with my loving bumbling fumble,
Found the whole world go black. The trap was shut.

Now in your juices, I
Am helpless to give warning to my rivals
And, worse, have to digest them when they die.

And worst, since now I'm one
Of your true converts, what is all my labour? —
To flaunt your signals in the shocking sun.

(*1969*)

Dionaea muscipula
Venus fly-trap

South-east United States

Ericaceae: Heather family

Ted Hughes

Heather

The upper millstone heaven
Grinds the heather's face hard and small.
Heather only toughens.

And out of a mica sterility
That nobody else wants
Thickens a nectar
Keen as adder venom.

A wind from the end of the sky
Buffs and curries the grizzly bear-dark pelt
Of long skylines
Browsing in innocence
Through their lasting purple aeons.

Heather is listening
Past hikers, gunshots, picnickers
For the star-drift
Of the returning ice.

No news here
But the crumbling outcrop voices
Of grouse.

A sea of bees, meanwhile, mapped by the sun.

(*1979*)

Calluna vulgaris
common, white or Scottish heather, ling

Europe, Asia Minor, naturalised in North America

Norman MacCaig

Bell Heather

People make songs about your big cousin
Extravagantly sprawled over mountain after mountain
They tear him up and he goes off to England
On the bumpers of cars, on shiny radiators.

But you're more beautiful and you blossom first,
In square feet and raggedy circles.
Your blue travels a hundred yards
That are a main road for bees.

If I were an adder, I'd choose you
For my royal palace. My sliding tongue
Would savour the thin scent
Of your boudoirs and banqueting halls.

A modest immodesty is a good thing,
Little blaze of blue on a rock face.
I'll try it myself. Will the bees come,
The wild bees, with their white noses?

(*1980*)

Erica cinerea
bell heather

Europe

Adrienne Rich

The Corpse-Plant

How dare a sick man, or an obedient man, write poems?
— Whitman

A milk-glass bowl hanging by three chains
from the discolored ceiling
is beautiful tonight. On the floor, leaves, crayons,
innocent dust foregather.

Neither obedient nor sick, I turn my head,
feeling the weight of a thick gold ring
in either lobe. I see the corpse-plants
clustered in a hobnailed tumbler

at my elbow, white as death, I'd say,
if I'd ever seen death;
whiter than life
next to my summer-stained hand.

Is it in the sun that truth begins?
Lying under that battering light
the first few hours of summer
I felt scraped clean, washed down

to ignorance. The gold in my ears,
souvenir of a shrewd old city,
might have been wearing thin as wires
found in the bones of a woman's head

miraculously kept in its essentials
in some hot cradle-tomb of time.
I felt my body slipping through
the fingers of its mind.

Later, I slid on wet rocks,
threw my shoes across a brook,
waded on algae-furred stones
to join them. That day I found

the corpse-plants, growing like
shadows on a negative
in the chill of fern and lichen-rust.
That day for the first time

I gave them their deathly names —
or did they name themselves? —
not 'Indian pipes' as once
we children knew them.

Tonight, I think of winter,
winters of mind, of flesh,
sickness of the rot-smell of leaves
turned silt-black, heavy as tarpaulin,

obedience of the elevator cage
lowering itself, crank by crank
into the mine-pit,
forced labor forcibly renewed —

but the horror is dimmed:
like the negative of one
intolerable photograph
it barely sorts itself out

under the radiance of the milk-glass shade.
Only death's insect whiteness
crooks its neck in a tumbler
where I placed its sign by choice.

(1963, *1966*)

Monotropa uniflora
Indian pipe

Himalayas, Japan, North and Central America

Ted Hughes

Rhododendrons

Dripped a chill virulence
Into my nape —
Rubberized prison-wear of suppression!

Guarding and guarded by
The Council's black
Forbidding forbidden stones.

The policeman's protected leaf!

Detestable evergreen sterility!
Over dead acid gardens
Where blue widows, shrined in Sunday, shrank

To arthritic clockwork,
Yapped like terriers and shook sticks from doorways
Vast and black and proper as museums.

Cenotaphs and the moor-silence!
Rhododendrons and rain!
It is all one. It is over.

Evergloom of official titivation —
Uniform at the reservoir, and the chapel,
And the graveyard park,

Ugly as a brass-band in India.

(*1979*)

Rhododendron spp.

China, Himalayas, South-east Asian and Malaysian mountains, New Guinea, Australia, Europe

Kathleen Jamie

Rhododendrons

They were brought under sail
from a red-tinged east,
carried down gangplanks
in dockers' arms. Innocent
and rare. Their thick leaves
bore a salt-damp gleam,
their blooms a hidden gargle
in their green throats.

Shuddering on trains
To Poolewe, or Arduine,
where the head gardener leaned
across the factor's desk. On a hill
above the sparkling loch
he spoke to his hands,
and terraces were cut,
sites marked, shallow holes dug

before they were turned out.
— Such terribly gentle
work, the grasping of the fat
glazed pots, the fertile
globe of the root-ball
undisturbed, Yunnan
or Himalayan earth
settled with them.

So we step out from their shade
to overlook Loch Melfort
and the bare glens, ready now
to claim this flowering, purple
flame-bright exotica as our own;
a commonplace, native
as language or living memory,
to our slightly acid soil.

(*1999*)

Ralph Waldo Emerson

The Rhodora

On Being Asked, Whence Is The Flower?

In May, when sea-winds pierced our solitudes,
I found the fresh Rhodora in the woods,
Spreading its leafless blooms in a damp nook,
To please the desert and the sluggish brook.
The purple petals, fallen in the pool,
Made the black water with their beauty gay;
Here might the red-bird come his plumes to cool,
And court the flower that cheapens his array.
Rhodora! if the sages ask thee why
This charm is wasted on the earth and sky,
Tell them, dear, that if eyes were made for seeing,
Then Beauty is its own excuse for being:
Why thou wert there, O rival of the rose!
I never thought to ask, I never knew;
But, in my simple ignorance, suppose
The self-same Power that brought me there brought you.

(1834, *1839*, *1847*)

Rhododendron canadense
rhodora

North-east North America

Euphorbiaceae: Spurge family

Dante Gabriel Rossetti

The Woodspurge

The wind flapped loose, the wind was still,
Shaken out dead from tree and hill:
I had walk'd on at the wind's will, —
I sat now, for the wind was still.

Between my knees my forehead was, —
My lips, drawn in, said not Alas!
My hair was over in the grass,
My naked ears heard the day pass.

My eyes, wide open, had the run
Of some ten weeds to fix upon;
Among those few, out of the sun,
The woodspurge flower'd, three cups in one.

From perfect grief there need not be
Wisdom or even memory:
One thing then learnt remains to me, —
The woodspurge has a cup of three.

(*1870*)

Euphorbia amygdaloides
woodspurge

Europe, South-west Asia

Fagaceae: Beech family

Jorie Graham

I Was Taught Three

names for the tree facing my window
almost within reach, elastic

with squirrels, memory banks, homes.
Castagno took itself to heart, its pods

like urchins clung to where they landed
claiming every bit of shadow

at the hem. *Chassagne*, on windier days,
nervous in taffeta gowns,

whispering, on the verge of being
anarchic, though well bred.

And then *chestnut*, whipped pale and clean
by all the inner reservoirs

called upon to do their even share of work.
It was not the kind of tree

got at by default — imagine that — not one
in which only the remaining leaf

was loyal. No, this
was all first person, and I

was the stem, holding within myself the whole
bouquet of three

at once given and received: smallest roadmaps
of coincidence. What is the idea

that governs blossoming? The human tree
clothed with its nouns, or this one

just outside my window promising more firmly
than can be

that it will reach my sill eventually, the leaves
silent as suppressed desires, and I

a name among them.

(*1980*)

Castanea sativa
chestnut

Mediterranean to the Caucasus; introduced to Britain by the Romans

James Lasdun

Oxblood

Mid-October, our Blackjack oak
Peppers the tar-paper roof with its ripened acorns;
Day and night, two weeks of it, Priapic
Scattershot clattering down
With every gust of wind from the mountain;
I stare outside. Impossible to sleep, think, work;

Into my mind a memory comes:
Another oak, the King Charles oak
That stood in our garden at home;
Survivor of summer lightning and winter storms,
The humps on its thick trunk bulging
Like muscles under the weight of its limbs.

One year half the buds withered
Before they'd opened. The rest stayed sickly yellow.
Oak-apples swelled on the twigs. Ringed ears of fungus
Sprouted from the scar of a lopped-off branch.
'Oxblood', the tree-doctor said,
And showed you where to dig it in.

The blood was granular, rich-smelling, moist, its crimson
Concentrated, masquerading as black:
I fingered it with a boy's
Professional interest in new substances:
Elixir of mud and fire; alchemic cack . . .
We dug it into the sloping lawn,

And waited — three years, four years,
Bad years, lithium years; lost jobs and breakdowns;
Your children's serial adolescence;
Once in a twilit hospital room
We watched your body sleeping on the bed;
Trespassers in the kingdom of the dead,

Bearing our modest gifts like ransom . . .
And then one spring the buds came strong again,
Lobed sprigs bubbling a haze, and like the stick
That blossomed when it stirred Medea's potion,
The tree burst into leaf again so thick
Its namesake could have hidden in its crown

All summer from his father's killers.
And I think of you now in your office, flourishing,
Bullish again, imperious, firing commands,
The silver claw-grip pencil firm in your hands,
Work warding off regret, age, doubt,
Catastrophe that stalks you through your friends,

Though if it should lay its regicidal axe
Against your neck, I think the cut would show
Not flesh but tree-rings circling back to zero,
And I wonder as I listen to this oak's
Triumphal drum, what sorceress filled your veins,
And who was the sacrificial ox.

(*1995*)

Quercus spp.
oak

Northern temperate regions, south to Malaysia and Colombia at altitude, Europe

Thomas Lynch

Loneliest of Trees, The Winter Oak

after Housman

Loneliest of trees, the winter oak
Still leafy here in bald November
Though withered still whispers 'Remember . . .
After All Hallows, All Saints, All Souls . . .'

Now of my three score years and ten
Fifty will not come again
And seventy autumns, less a score,
It only leaves me twenty more.

And since twenty winters aren't enough
To contemplate the taking of our leaves,
About the woods I'll go and gather such
Lessons as there are in fallen leaves.

(*1998*)

Paul Lawrence Dunbar

The Haunted Oak

Pray why are you so bare, so bare,
  Oh, bough of the old oak-tree;
And why, when I go through the shade you throw,
  Runs a shudder over me?

My leaves are green as the best, I trow,
  And sap ran free in my veins,
But I saw in the moonlight dim and weird
  A guiltless victim's pains.

I bent me down to hear his sigh;
  I shook with his gurgling moan,
And I trembled sore when they rode away,
  And left him here alone.

They'd charged him with the old, old crime,
  And set him fast in jail:
Oh, why does the dog howl all night long,
  And why does the night wind wail?

He prayed his prayer and he swore his oath,
  And he raised his hand to the sky;
But the beat of hoofs smote on his ear,
  And the steady tread drew nigh.

Who is it rides by night, by night,
  Over the moonlit road?
And what is the spur that keeps the pace,
  What is the galling goad?

And now they beat at the prison door,
  'Ho, keeper, do no stay!
We are friends of him whom you hold within,
  And we fain would take him away

'From those who ride fast on our heels
  With mind to do him wrong;
They have no care for his innocence,
  And the rope they bear is long.'

They have fooled the jailer with lying words,
  They have fooled the man with lies;

The bolts unbar, the locks are drawn,
  And the great door open flies

Now they have taken him from the jail,
  And hard and fast they ride,
And the leader laughs low down in his throat,
  As they halt my trunk beside.

Oh, the judge, he wore a mask of black,
  And the doctor one of white,
And the minister, with his oldest son,
  Was curiously bedight.

Oh, foolish man, why weep you now?
  'Tis but a little space,
And the time will come when these shall dread
  The mem'ry of your face.

I feel the rope against my bark,
  And the weight of him in my grain,
I feel in the throe of his final woe
  The touch of my own last pain.

And never more shall leaves come forth
  On a bough that bears the ban;
I am burned with dread, I am dried and dead,
  From the curse of a guiltless man.

And ever the judge rides by, rides by,
  And goes to hunt the deer,
And ever another rides his soul
  In the guise of a mortal fear.

And ever the man he rides me hard,
  And never a night stays he;
For I feel his curse as a haunted bough,
  On the trunk of a haunted tree.

(*1903*)

Walt Whitman

'I Saw in Louisiana a Live-Oak Growing'

I saw in Louisiana a live-oak growing,
All alone stood it and the moss hung down from the branches,
Without any companion it grew there uttering joyous leaves of
  dark green,
And its look, rude, unbending, lusty, made me think of myself,
But I wonder'd how it could utter joyous leaves standing alone
  there without its friend near, for I knew I could not,
And I broke off a twig with a certain number of leaves upon it,
  and twined around it a little moss,
And brought it away, and I have placed it in sight in my room,
It is not needed to remind me as of my own dear friends,
(For I believe lately I think of little else than of them,)
Yet it remains to me a curious token, it makes me think of
  manly love;
For all that, and though the live-oak glistens there in Louisiana
  solitary in a wide flat space,
Uttering joyous leaves all its life without a friend a lover near,
I know very well I could not.

(*1860*)

Quercus virginiana
live-oak

South-east United States

Eric Ormsby

Live Oak, with Bromeliads

The live oak tufted with bromeliads
By the salt lagoon looks almost scarred.
Airplants bristle on its grey
Limbs like knotted sprigs of surgeon's thread.
In sprawling notches of the canopy
Spanish moss dangles in snarled clusters
While the long sunshine of Miami's winter
Lends it a gloss of fractured malachite.

But nothing could be less wounded than this oak.
Its knuckled roots infiltrate the dank
Marsh of the hammock, they drink the sand
Riddled by land-crabs to a moon-pocked surface.
And look:
                like praying candles in a smoky shrine
Set up to honour the salt god of the marsh,
The ranked branches embrace their parasites.

(*1992*)

Gentianaceae: Gentian family

Medbh McGuckian

Gentians

In my alpine house, the slavery I pay
My wilful gentians! exploring all their pleats
And tucks as though they had something precious
Deep inside, that beard of camel-hair
In the throat. I watch them
Ease their heads so slowly
Through their thumbhole necklines, till they sit
Like tailors in their earth shoes,
Their watery husband's knots. No insects
Visit them, nor do their ovaries swell,
Yet every night in Tibet their seeds
Are membraned by the snow, their roots
Are bathed by the passage of melt-water;
They tease like sullen spinsters
The dewfall of summer limes.

(1982)

Gentiana spp.
gentian

Temperate regions of Europe, Asia, China and Australasia, and the Arctic

Emily Dickinson

'The Gentian Has a Parched Corolla' [1424]

The Gentian has a parched Corolla —
Like azure dried
'Tis Nature's buoyant juices
Beatified —
Without a vaunt or sheen
As casual as Rain
And as benign —

When most is past — it comes —
Nor isolate it seems
Its Bond its Friend —
To fill its Fringed career
And aid an aged Year
Abundant end —

Its lot — were it forgot —
This Truth endear —
Fidelity is gain
Creation o'er —

(*c.* 1877, *1945*)

D. H. Lawrence

Bavarian Gentians

Not every man has gentians in his house
in soft September, at slow, sad Michaelmas.

Bavarian gentians, tall and dark, but dark
darkening the daytime torch-like with the smoking blueness of Pluto's gloom,
ribbed hellish flowers erect, with their blaze of darkness spread blue,
blown flat into points, by the heavy white draught of the day.

Torch-flowers of the blue-smoking darkness, Pluto's dark-blue blaze
black lamps from the halls of Dis, smoking dark blue
giving off darkness, blue darkness, upon Demeter's yellow-pale day
Whom have you come for, here in the white-cast day?

Reach me a gentian, give me a torch!
let me guide myself with the blue, forked torch of a flower
down the darker and darker stairs, where blue is darkened on blueness
down the way Persephone goes, just now, in first-frosted September
to the sightless realm where darkness is married to dark
and Persephone herself is but a voice, as a bride
a gloom invisible enfolded in the deeper dark
of the arms of Pluto as he ravishes her once again
and pierces her once more with his passion of the utter dark
among the splendour of black-blue torches, shedding fathomless darkness on the nuptials.

Give me a flower on a tall stem, and three dark flames,
for I will go to the wedding, and be wedding-guest
at the marriage of the living dark.

(1928–9, *1932*)

Gentiana bavaria
Bavarian gentian

Europe

Geraniaceae: Geranium family

D. H. Lawrence

Red Geranium and Godly Mignonette

Imagine that any mind ever *thought* a red geranium!
As if the redness of a red geranium could be anything but a
  sensual experience
and as if sensual experience could take place before there were
  any senses.
We know that even God could not imagine the redness of a red
  geranium
nor the smell of mignonette
when the geraniums were not, and mignonette neither.
And even when they were, even God would have to have a nose
to smell at the mignonette.
You can't imagine the Holy Ghost sniffing at cherry-pie
  heliotrope.
Or the Most High, during the coal age, cudgelling his mighty
  brains
even if he had any brains: straining his mighty brains
to think, among the moss and mud of lizards and mastodons
to think out, in the abstract, when all was twilit green and
  muddy:
'Now there shall be tum-tiddly-um, and tum-tiddly-um,
hey-presto! scarlet geranium!'
We know it couldn't be done.
But imagine, among the mud and the mastodons

God sighing and yearning with tremendous creative yearning, in
  that dark green mess
oh, for some other beauty, some other beauty
that blossomed at last, red geranium, and mignonette.

(1928–9, *1932*)

Pelargonium spp.
geranium
Mostly southern Africa, also east Mediterranean to Iraq, Saudi Arabia, St Helena, Tristan da Cunha, south India, Australia and New Zealand

Reseda odorata
Resedaceae (Mignonette family)
mignonette
North Africa

Theodore Roethke

The Geranium

When I put her out, once, by the garbage pail,
She looked so limp and bedraggled,
So foolish and trusting, like a sick poodle,
Or a wizened aster in late September,
I brought her back in again
For a new routine —
Vitamins, water, and whatever
Sustenance seemed sensible
At the time: she'd lived
So long on gin, bobbie pins, half-smoked cigars, dead beer,
Her shriveled petals falling
On the faded carpet, the stale
Steak grease stuck to her fuzzy leaves.
(Dried-out, she creaked like a tulip.)

The things she endured! —
The dumb dames shrieking half the night
Or the two of us, alone, both seedy,
Me breathing booze at her,
She leaning out of her pot toward the window.

Near the end, she seemed almost to hear me —
And that was scary —
So when that snuffling cretin of a maid
Threw her, pot and all, into the trash-can,
I said nothing.

But I sacked the presumptuous hag the next week,
I was that lonely.

(*1963*)

Ginkgoaceae: Ginkgo family

Howard Nemerov

Ginkgoes in Fall

They are the oldest living captive race,
Primitive gymnosperms that in the wild
Are rarely found or never, temple trees
Brought down in line unbroken from the deep
Past where the Yellow Emperor lies tombed.

Their fallen yellow fruit mimics the scent
Of human vomit, the definitive statement of
An attitude, and their translucency of leaf,
Filtering a urinary yellow light,
Remarks a delicate wasting of the world,

An innuendo to be clarified
In winter when they defecate their leaves
And bear the burden of their branches up
Alone and bare, dynastic diagrams
Of their distinguished genealogies.

(*1977*)

Ginkgo biloba
maidenhair tree

East China

Gramineae: Grass family

John Clare

The Wheat Ripening

What time the wheat-field tinges rusty brown
And barley bleaches in its mellow grey
'Tis sweet some smooth mown baulk to wander down
Or cross the fields on footpath's narrow way
Just in the mealy light of waking day.
As glittering dewdrops moist the maiden's gown
And sparkling bounces from her nimble feet
Journeying to milking from the neighbouring town,
Making life light with song; and it is sweet
To mark the grazing herds and list the clown
Urge on his ploughing team with cheering calls,
And merry shepherds whistling toils begun,
And hoarse-tongued bird-boy whose unceasing brawls
Join the lark's ditty to the rising sun.

(1821–4, *1908*)

Triticum spp.
wheat

Mediterranean, Europe to Iran

Vikram Seth

Evening Wheat

Evening is the best time for wheat.
Toads croak.
Children ride buffaloes home for supper.
The last loads are shoulder-borne.
Squares light up
And the wheat sags with a late gold.
There on the other side of the raised path
Is the untransplanted emerald rice.
But it is the wheat I watch, the still dark gold
With maybe a pig that has strayed from the brigade
Enjoying a few soft ears.

(*1985*)

Hyacinthaceae: Hyacinth family

Emily Brontë

'The Blue Bell is the Sweetest Flower'

The blue bell is the sweetest flower
That waves in summer air
Its blossoms have the mightiest power
To soothe my spirit's care

There is a spell in purple heath
Too wildly, sadly drear
The violet has a fragrant breath
But fragrance will not cheer

The trees are bare, the sun is cold
And seldom, seldom seen —
The heavens have lost their zone of gold
The earth its robe of green

And ice upon the glancing stream
Has cast its sombre shade
And distant hills and valleys seem
In frozen mist arrayed —

The blue bell cannot charm me now
The heath has lost its bloom
The violets in the glen below
They yield no sweet perfume

But though I mourn the heather-bell
'Tis better far, away
I know how fast my tears would swell
To see it smile today

And that wood flower that hides so shy
Beneath the mossy stone
Its balmy scent and dewy eye
'Tis not for them I moan

It is the slight and stately stem
The blossom's silvery blue
The buds hid like a sapphire gem
In sheaths of emerald hue

'Tis these that breathe upon my heart
A calm and softening spell
That if it makes the tear-drop start
Has power to soothe as well

For these I weep, so long divided
Through winter's dreary day
In longing weep — but most when guided
On withered banks to stray

If chilly then the light should fall
Adown the dreary sky
And gild the dank and darkened wall
With transient brilliancy

How do I yearn, how do I pine
For the time of flowers to come
And turn me from that fading shine
To mourn the fields of home —

(*c.* 1840, *1923*)

Hyacinthoides non-scripta
bluebell

West Europe

Kathleen Jamie

Speirin

Binna feart, hinny,
yin day we'll gang thegither
tae thae stourie
blaebellwids,
and lose wirsels —

see, I'd raither
whummel a single oor
intae the blae o thae wee flo'ers

than live fur a' eternity
in some cauld hivvin.

Wheest, nou, till I spier o ye
will ye haud wi me?

Proposal

Don't be scared, honey,
one day we'll go together
to the dusty
bluebell-woods
and lose ourselves —

see, I'd rather
tumble for a single hour
into the blue of those little flowers
than live for all eternity
in some cold heaven.

Hush now, let me ask you
will you hold with me?

(*2001*)

Hydrangeaceae: Hydrangea family

Moniza Alvi

Hydrangeas

The hydrangeas are massing
in gardens cherished by aunts.
Grimly ornamental, by tiled paths
they insist there is one garden —
theirs,
and if cats dare piss there
they swallow them
in huge mauve mouthfuls.

The hydrangeas are massing
heavy as cannonballs.
Guarding the house
they hiss to themselves
secretly.

They'll plan their own wedding —
invite no bride or groom.

(*1993*)

Hydrangea spp.
hydrangea

Himalayas to Japan and the Philippines

Louise Glück

Mock Orange

It is not the moon, I tell you.
It is these flowers
lighting the yard.

I hate them.
I hate them as I hate sex,
the man's mouth
sealing my mouth, the man's
paralyzing body —

and the cry that always escapes,
the low, humiliating
premise of union —

In my mind tonight
I hear the question and pursuing answer
fused in one sound
that mounts and mounts and then
is split into the old selves,
the tired antagonisms. Do you see?
We were made fools of.
And the scent of mock orange
drifts through the window.

How can I rest?
How can I be content
while there is still
that odor in the world?

(*1985*)

Philadelphus coronarius
mock orange

Europe, south-west Asia

Iridaceae: Iris family

Louise Glück

The Wild Iris

At the end of my suffering
there was a door.

Hear me out: that which you call death
I remember.

Overhead, noises, branches of the pine shifting.
Then nothing. The weak sun
flickered over the dry surface.

It is terrible to survive
as consciousness
buried in the dark earth.

Then it was over: that which you fear, being
a soul and unable
to speak, ending abruptly, the stiff earth
bending a little. And what I took to be
birds darting in low shrubs.

You who do not remember
passage from the other world
I tell you I could speak again: whatever
returns from oblivion returns
to find a voice:

from the center of my life came
a great fountain, deep blue
shadows on azure seawater.

(*1992*)

Iris spp.
iris

Eurasia, North Africa, North America

'Michael Field'
(Katherine Harris Bradley and Edith Emma Cooper)

Irises

In a vase of gold
And scarlet, how cold
The flicker of wrinkled grays
In this iris-sheaf! My eyes fill with wonder
At the tossed, moist light, at the withered scales under
And among the uncertain sprays.

The wavings of white
On the cloudy light,
And the finger-marks of pearl;
The facets of crystal, the golden feather,
The ways that the petals fold over together,
The way that the buds unfurl!

(*1893*)

Ted Hughes

Sketch of a Goddess

We have one Iris. A Halberd
Of floral complications. Two blooms are full,
Floppily opened, or undone rather.
                                                            Royal
Seraglio twin sisters, contending
For the Sultan's eye. Even here
One is superior.
Rivalry has devastated
Everything about them except
The womb's temptation and offer.

That one's past it. But this one's in her prime.
She utters herself
Utterly into appeal. A surrender
Of torn mucous membranes, veined and purpled,
A translucence of internal organs
In a frisson,
Torn open,
The core debauched,
All loosely dangling helplessness
And enfolding claspers —

Delicately holding herself
As if every edge were cringing round a nerve.

Actually
She's lolling her tongue right out,
Her uvula arched,
Her uterus everted —

An overpowered bee buries its face
In the very beard of her ovaries.

It deafens itself
In a dreadful belly-cry — just out of human hearing.

(*1986*)

Labiatae: Mint family

Louise Glück

Lamium

This is how you live when you have a cold heart.
As I do: in shadows, trailing over cool rock,
under the great maple trees.

The sun hardly touches me.
Sometimes I see it in early spring, rising very far away.
Then leaves grow over it, completely hiding it. I feel it
glinting through the leaves, erratic,
like someone hitting the side of a glass with a metal spoon.

Living things don't all require
light in the same degree. Some of us
make our own light: a silver leaf
like a path no one can use, a shallow
lake of silver in the darkness under the great maples.

But you know this already.
You and the others who think
you live for truth and, by extension, love
all that is cold.

(*1992*)

Lamium spp.
white dead nettle

Eurasia, naturalised eastern North America

Seamus Heaney

Mint

It looked like a clump of small dusty nettles
Growing wild at the gable of the house
Beyond where we dumped our refuse and old bottles:
Unverdant ever, almost beneath notice.

But, to be fair, it also spelled promise
And newness in the backyard of our life
As if something callow yet tenacious
Sauntered in green alleys and grew rife.

The snip of scissor blades, the light of Sunday
Mornings when the mint was cut and loved:
My last things will be first things slipping from me.
Yet let all things go free that have survived.

Let smells of mint go heady and defenceless
Like inmates liberated in that yard.
Like the disregarded ones we turned against
Because we'd failed them by our disregard.

(*1996*)

Mentha spp.
mint

Temperate regions of the Old World

Lorna Goodison

A Bed of Mint

A bed of mint
beneath the window
of the room where we sleep
will render the morning air
sharp and sweet.

I'd turn to you in my sleep
half out of dreams
murmuring 'Whose bed
is it that smells of mint?'
'Ours' you will whisper.

Then we will roll over
like the waves and wake
to draw tea from the source
springing beneath the window,
living mint and sweet to each other.

(*2000*)

Robert Herrick

The Rosemarie branch

Grow for two ends, it matters not at all,
Be't for my *Bridall*, or my *Buriall.*

(*1648*)

Rosmarinus officinalis
rosemary

Europe and the Mediterranean

Marianne Moore

Rosemary

Beauty and Beauty's son and rosemary —
Venus and Love, her son, to speak plainly —
born of the sea supposedly,
at Christmas each, in company,
braids a garland of festivity.
    Not always rosemary —

since the flight to Egypt, blooming differently.
With lancelike leaf, green but silver underneath,
its flowers — white originally —
turned blue. The herb of memory,
imitating the blue robe of Mary,
    is not too legendary

to flower both as symbol and as pungency.
Springing from stones beside the sea,
the height of Christ when thirty-three —
it feeds on dew and to the bee
'hath a dumb language'; is in reality
    a kind of Christmas-tree.

(*1968*)

Richard Wilbur

Thyme Flowering Among Rocks

This, if Japanese,
Would represent grey boulders
Walloped by rough seas

So that, here or there,
The balked water tossed its froth
Straight into the air.

Here, where things are what
They are, it is thyme blooming,
Rocks, and nothing but —

Having, nonetheless,
Many small leaves implicit,
A green countlessness.

Crouching down, peering
Into perplexed recesses,
You find a clearing

Occupied by sun
Where, along prone, rachitic
Branches, one by one,

Pale stems arise, squared
In the manner of *Mentha*,
The oblong leaves paired.

One branch, in ending,
Lifts a little and begets
A straight-ascending

Spike, whorled with fine blue
Or purple trumpets, banked in
The leaf-axils. You

Are lost now in dense
Fact, fact which one might have thought
Hidden from the sense,

Blinking at detail
Peppery as this fragrance,
Lost to proper scale

As, in the motion
Of stripped fins, a bathysphere
Forgets the ocean.

It makes the craned head
Spin. Unfathomed thyme! The world's
A dream, Basho said,

Not because that dream's
A falsehood, but because it's
Truer than it seems.

(*1969*)

Thymus vulgaris
thyme

West Mediterranean to south-east Italy

Lauraceae: Laurel family

Seni Seneviratne

Cinnamon Roots

Cinnamon sweet wood spice
once traded like gold
when I look for my roots
I find you yellowish brown
like my winter skin
native of Sri Lanka
growing wild in the jungles
of the Kandy Highlands

1492 Columbus never finds you
sailing westwards to the lands
of the Arawak Indians
he promises spices and gold
trophies for a Spanish Queen
brings her Taino slaves as 'gifts'

But Portugal travels East
to an island that falls like
a teardrop from the tip of India
finds your soft sweetness
wraps it in hard cash
grows rich on your rarity
founding a spice trade
that deals in blood

The Dutch make plantations
tame your wild fragrance
that can never sweeten their breath
demand quotas of your bark
enforced by death and torture
burn down your August harvest
fabled fuel of the phoenix fire
to keep up the prices

Dutch East India
becomes British East India
your acres grow in the rain
and heat of Sri Lanka
filling the coffers
of the British Empire

1992 I buy your ground aroma
in pre-packed jars fry you
with aubergines and coriander
look for my roots
find you yellowish brown
like my winter skin
native of Sri Lanka
growing wild in the jungles
of the Kandy Highlands

(*1993*)

Cinnamomum zeylanicum
cinnamon

Sri Lanka and south-west India

Mildmay Fane, Earl of Westmorland

Occasioned by Seeing a Walk of Bay-trees

No Thunder blasts *Jove's* Plant, nor can
Misfortune warp an honest Man;
Shaken He may be, by some one
Or other Gust, Unleav'd by none:
Though tribulation's sharp and keen,
His Resolutions keep Green;
And whilst Integrity's his wall,
His Year's all Spring, and hath no Fall.

(*1648*)

Laurus nobilis
bay

Mediterranean

Christopher Middleton

Avocado Plant

How good it was
to burst from the nut
now my roots dangle in clear water

white roots trailing gripped by little turrets
cockfeather cloud I plant in ears
a sting of wind

yet nothing shakes me from the split
nut held in the mouth of the bottle
and my sixteen leaves shot from the tendril

quilts pointed at either end
and oval
only hatch these tufts of shadow

flicked across the wall as I climb forever
out of myself on the sunbaked zinc
casing of an old water-fan

(*1975*)

Persea americana
avocado

Central America

Leguminosae: Pea family

Jack Mapanje

The Acacias of Gaborone City, Botswana

When I first saw these acacias of Gaborone
I flinched at their stubborn roots once harshly
shattered by the cruel bombs of apartheid,

I wondered why their leaves insolently opened
up when their brute branches and keen thorns
tore our careless hands as the brown sparrows

Teasingly hopped about the creamy flowers;
I feared how their grey blended with our hazy
landscapes too and wished their jacarandas were

Likewise fabricated to shield our barrenscapes;
but today when I watched this capital branching
in all directions and like other world capital cities

Quietly breeding dual carriageways, I sighed
at their latent malignancies as the chirruping
sparrows succumbed to the countless car alarms

Tweeting from house to hut; even you thought
of planting more acacia trees around your house —
to scratch some thief to shame! you despaired.

(*1998*)

Acacia spp.
acacia

Tropics, especially Australia

Basil du Toit

Thorn Trees

Axes thud on them all day
for barricades and firewood.
The wood fractures messily, hinging itself
at the breaks with tough hempen elbows.

The bark isn't made for easily sloughing
or fissured with menstrual heaviness;
it's fainter, more like a *trompe l'oeil* skin
applied straight onto the wood.

When summer vegetation stands high and dry,
squeaking like derelict water pumps,
and cicadas protract their skewering noise,
the thorn waits beside skulls and horns.

For a few days in spring
other trees rut with their obvious blossoms
but a fine, green lace blurs the thorn
and issues a noticeable, dry perfume.

Now goats rear cautiously against the trees,
one forefoot drooping daintily,
and twist their heads into a basket of thorns
to sample the scented needlework.

(*1992*)

Acacia paradoxa
thorn tree

Temperate Australia

John Clare

Beans in Blossom

The south-west wind! how pleasant in the face
It breathes! while, sauntering in a musing pace,
I roam these new ploughed fields; or by the side
Of this old wood, where happy birds abide,
And the rich blackbird, through his golden bill,
Utters wild music when the rest are still.
Luscious the scent comes of the blossomed bean,
As o'er the path in rich disorder lean
Its stalks; when bees, in busy rows and toils,
Load home luxuriantly their yellow spoils.
The herd-cows toss the molehills in their play;
And often stand the stranger's steps at bay,
Mid clover blossoms red and tawny white,
Strong scented with the summer's warm delight.

(1824–32, *1835*)

Vicia faba
broad bean, field bean, horse bean
Usually considered to be a cultigen derived from *Vicia narbonensis*

Mediterranean to Central Asia

Lorna Goodison

About the Tamarind

Under strict dry conditions I can grow as high
as eighty feet and my open frame half as wide.
Then my trunk which yields a kind of timber
called by some the mahogany of Madeira
will become too substantial and stout for you
to wrap your short arms around.

My crown, a mass of fine light green foliage,
pinate leaves, which dip gracefully to shade you
fold in upon themselves at night, private.
I bloom small gold flowers which appear
to bleed the gold of guinea and the blood
drawn by the lash of slavery.

I am slow growing, rooted deep, resisting
breeze blow, hot air and hurricane winds.
I flourish even in rocky terrain with little or no
cultural attention. My cinnamon brown pods
grow in profusion, I bear long, I bear abundance
and Pharoahs ate of me.

Tamir Hindi the Persian poet chanted under my shade.
Rooted first in Africa, transplanted wherever
I can thrive, that is wherever there is sun of life.
I require his constant kiss in order to flourish.
His hot caresses I absorb and return in the form
of fire purifying, all-consuming.

Tamarindus Indica, native of Africa, from root
to leaftip, my every part has been employed
to meet human need. Consider how they eat
my flowers and leaves, roast my seeds, pound them
into paste for sizing. My fruit which is sometimes sour
can be sugared into tamarind balls, symbols of slavery.

Sometimes in alluvial soil I grow large and sweet,
that is in places where I am valued and needed.
Then I heal, refrigerant for fevers, I am laxative.
I work alone or can combine with juice of limes
or extrusion of bees, together we can cure
bilious digestive systems large as that of elephants.

I reduce swellings, loosen the grip of paralysis,
and return the drunken inebriated on illusion,
the cheap coarse wine of the world, to sobriety
perhaps to become one day truly drunk like me
with the wine unseen, which causes me to sway
so that the unannointed mock me.

In Africa they soak my bark with corn
and feed this to domestic birds in the belief
that if they stray or are stolen they will return.
In Asia, a little tamarind and coconut milk
is placed at the mouths of infants as their first drink,
the world's initial welcoming libation.

And the elephant's long memory is aided by the eating
of my bark and the pods, flesh and seeds of my fruit.
My leaves give soothing bush baths for rashes or the cut
of the tamarind whip. The correction and the cure
both come from me. There are people who claim
I am dwelling place of the spirit of rain.

I raise the temperature in my immediate vicinity
so the cold-hearted fear me. I will tell you now
why few plants grow wild beneath me and why
you should not use me as policetree to tether your horse.
Because I have not come to rule over, overpower
vanquish, conquer or constrain anyone.

I provide the mordant in dyes, burn me for charcoal
I rise as insense. My sapwood is pale and golden.
My heartwood though is royal purple and earth brown,
I am high and low all at once. Sour and sweet,
I came with the enslaved across the seas to bear for you
when force-ripe capricious crops fail.

I bear. Not even the salt of the ocean can stunt me.
Plant me on abiding rock or foaming restless waters.
Set me in burying grounds, I will shade the ancestors.

O bitter weed and dry-heart tree, wait for me to bow.
I hope you can wait. Rest in Peace, Arawaks.
I am still here, still bearing after 400 years.

(*2000*)

Tamarindus indica
tamarind

Probable origin: tropical Africa

Emily Dickinson

'There is a Flower that Bees Prefer' [380]

There is a flower that Bees prefer —
And Butterflies — desire —
To gain the Purple Democrat
The Humming Bird — aspire —

And Whatsoever Insect pass —
A Honey bear away
Proportioned to his several dearth
And her — capacity —

Her face be rounder than the Moon
And ruddier than the Gown
Of Orchis in the Pasture —
Or Rhododendron — worn —

She doth not wait for June —
Before the World be Green —
Her sturdy little Countenance —
Against the Wind — be seen —

Contending with the Grass —
Near Kinsman to Herself —
For privilege of Sod and Sun —
Sweet Litigants for Life —

And when the Hills be full —
And newer fashions blow —
Doth not retract a single spice
For pang of jealousy —

Her Public — be the Noon —
Her Providence — the Sun —
Her Progress — by the Bee — proclaimed —
In sovereign — Swerveless Tune —

The Bravest — of the Host —
Surrendering — the last —
Nor even of Defeat — aware —
When cancelled by the Frost —

(*c.* 1862, *1890*)

Trifolium pratense
red or purple clover

Europe to Afghanistan, naturalised in North America

John Clare

To a Red Clover Blossom

Sweet bottle-shaped flower of lushy red,
  Born when the summer wakes her warmest breeze,
Among the meadow's waving grasses spread,
  Or 'neath the shade of hedge or clumping trees,
Bowing on slender stem thy heavy head;
  In sweet delight I view thy summer bed,
And list the drone of heavy humble-bees
  Along thy honey'd garden gaily led,
Down corn-field, striped balks, and pasture-leas.
  Fond warmings of the soul, that long have fled,
Revive my bosom with their kindlings still,
  As I bend musing o'er thy ruddy pride;
Recalling days when, dropt upon a hill,
  I cut my oaten trumpets by thy side.

(1819–21, *1821*)

Seamus Heaney

Whinlands

All year round the whin
Can show a blossom or two
But it's in full bloom now.
As if the small yolk stain

From all the birds' eggs in
All the nests of the spring
Were spiked and hung
Everywhere on bushes to ripen.

Hills oxidize gold.
Above the smoulder of green shoot
And dross of dead thorns underfoot
The blossoms scald.

Put a match under
Whins, they go up of a sudden.
They make no flame in the sun
But a fierce heat tremor

Yet incineration like that
Only takes the thorn.
The tough sticks don't burn,
Remain like bone, charred horn.

Gilt, jaggy, springy, frilled
This stunted, dry richness
Persists on hills, near stone ditches,
Over flintbed and battlefield.

(*1969*)

Ulex europaeus
gorse, whin

Heathland of Atlantic Europe; now weedy elsewhere, and a pest in New Zealand

Michael Longley

Gorse Fires

Cattle out of their byres are dungy still, lambs
Have stepped from last year as from an enclosure.
Five or six men stand gazing at a rusty tractor
Before carrying implements to separate fields.

I am travelling from one April to another.
It is the same train between the same embankments.
Gorse fires are smoking, but primroses burn
And celandines and white may and gorse flowers.

(*1991*)

Chris Orsman

Ornamental Gorse

It's ornamental where it's been
self-sown across the hogback,

obsequious and buttery,
cocking a snook at scars,

yellowing our quaint history
of occupation and reprise.

The spiny tangential crotch,
gullied and decorative,

I love from a distance,
a panorama over water

from lakeside to peninsula
where it's delicate in hollows,

or a topiary under heavens
cropped by the south wind.

I offer this crown of thorns
for the pity of my countrymen

unconvinced of the beauty
of their reluctant emblem: this

burnt, hacked, blitzed
exotic.

(*1994*)

Liliaceae: Lily family

Anne Ridler

Snakeshead Fritillaries

Some seedlings shoulder the earth away
Like Milton's lion plunging to get free,
Demanding notice. Delicate rare fritillary,
You enter creeping, like the snake
You're named for, and lay your ear to the ground.
The soundless signal comes, to arch the neck —
Losing the trampled look —
Follow the code for colour, whether
White or freckled with purple and pale,
A chequered dice-box tilted over the soil,
The yellow dice held at the base.

When light slants before the sunset, this is
The proper time to watch fritillaries.
They enter creeping; you go on your knees,
The flowers level with your eyes,
And catch the dapple of sunlight through the petals.

(*1994*)

Fritillaria meleagris
guinea flower

Europe, west Asia; naturalised in Britain (a protected species), though not recorded before 1732

James Reiss

Lily

Went out & scissored a lily, brought her inside
to study her fuzzy brown anthers loaded

with pollen, her needle-thin pistil & filaments
down to her ovary. Noted her sepals

were dotted with droplets; her waxy gold petals
were stippled with pigment, the comeliest rust spots,

like freckles on the face of a tomboy agog
in a tree house at twilight. Saw how, twice-dappled

with drizzle & beauty marks, she tilted a bit in her vase
toward my pencil as if she could lift it to write

& tell me the checkered tall story of all things in bloom.
Saw two of her petals were nibbled — by a rabbit? a fawn?

Wrote how she told me she loathed the incessant devouring
mouths which would strip her & call her a woman.

(*1998*)

Lilium canadense
lily

Eastern North America

Robert Herrick

How Lillies Came White

White though ye be; yet, Lillies, know,
From the first ye were not so:
        But Ile tell ye
        What befell ye;
Cupid and his Mother lay
In a Cloud; while both did play,
He with his pretty fingers prest
The rubie niplet of her breast;
Out of which, the creame of light,
        Like to a Dew,
        Fell downe on you
        And made ye white.

(*1648*)

Lilium candidum
Madonna lily, Bourbon lily

Balkans (possibly naturalised), Lebanon, Palestine/Israel
Figures in Cretan frescos 5,000 years old and has been cultivated since at least 1500 BC; possibly the Rose of Sharon of the Bible, and long associated with the Virgin Mary; cultivated in Britain by the fifteenth century — the only species known to Shakespeare

William Blake

The Lilly

The modest Rose puts forth a thorn:
The humble Sheep a threatning horn:
While the Lilly white, shall in Love delight,
Nor a thorn nor a threat stain her beauty bright.

(*1794*)

Mary Tighe

The Lily

May, 1809

How withered, perished seems the form
  Of yon obscure unsightly root!
Yet from the blight of wintry storm,
  It hides secure the precious fruit.

The careless eye can find no grace,
  No beauty in the scaly folds,
Nor see within the dark embrace
  What latent loveliness it holds.

Yet in that bulb, those sapless scales,
  The lily weeps her silver vest,
'Till vernal suns and vernal gales
  Shall kiss once more her pregnant breast.

Yes, hide beneath the mouldering heap
  The undelighting slighted thing;
There in the cold earth buried deep,
  In silence let it wait the spring.

Oh! many a stormy night shall close
  In gloom upon the barren earth,
While still, in undisturbed repose,
  Uninjured lies the future birth;

And Ignorance, with sceptic eye,
  Hope's patient smile shall wondering view;
Or mock her fond credulity,
  As her soft tears the spot bedew.

Sweet tear of hope, delicious tear!
  The sun, the shower indeed shall come;
The promised verdant shoot appear,
  And nature bid her blossoms bloom.

And thou, O virgin Queen of Spring!
  Shalt, from thy dark and lowly bed,
Bursting thy green sheath's silken string,
  Unveil thy charms, and perfume shed;

Unfold thy robes of purest white,
  Unsullied from their darksome grave,
And thy soft petals silvery light
  In the mild breeze unfettered wave.

So Faith shall seek the lowly dust
  Where humble Sorrow loves to lie,
And bid her thus her hopes entrust,
  And watch with patient, cheerful eye;

And bear the long, cold, wintry night,
  And bear her own degraded doom,
And wait till Heaven's reviving light,
  Eternal Spring! shall burst the gloom.

(*1811*)

Emily Dickinson

'Through the Dark Sod — As Education' [392]

Through the Dark Sod — as Education —
The Lily passes sure —
Feels her white foot — no trepidation —
Her faith — no fear —

Afterward — in the Meadow —
Swinging her Beryl Bell —
The Mold-life — all forgotten — now —
In Ecstasy — and Dell —

(*c.* 1892, *1929*)

Robert Herrick

To a Bed of Tulips

1. Bright Tulips, we do know,
   You had your comming hither;
   And Fading-time do's show,
   That Ye must quickly wither.

2. Your *Sister-hoods* may stay,
   And smile here for your houre,
   But dye ye must away:
   Even as the meanest Flower.

3. Come Virgins then, and see
   Your frailties; and bemone ye;
   For lost like these, 'twill be,
   As Time had never known ye.

(*1648*)

Tulipa spp.
tulip

Eurasia, east and central Asia, North Africa; cultivated in Iran since the thirteenth century when there were multicoloured forms; introduced via Turkey (not grown there before 1500, but prominent in design) to Europe (Vienna) in 1554; arrived in Holland in 1571, leading to 'tulipomania' (1634) with great financial speculation in bulbs, especially those 'Rembrandt' tulips with 'broken' flowers (i.e. infested with an aphid-transmitted virus)

E. J. Scovell

Deaths of Flowers

I would if I could choose
Age and die outwards as a tulip does;
Not as this iris drawing in, in-coiling
Its complex strange taut inflorescence, willing
Itself a bud again — though all achieved is
No more than a clenched sadness,

The tears of gum not flowing.
I would choose the tulip's reckless way of going;
Whose petals answer light, altering by fractions
From closed to wide, from one through many perfections,
Till wrecked, flamboyant, strayed beyond recall,
Like flakes of fire they piecemeal fall.

(*1988*)

Sylvia Plath

Tulips

The tulips are too excitable, it is winter here.
Look how white everything is, how quiet, how snowed-in.
I am learning peacefulness, lying by myself quietly
As the light lies on these white walls, this bed, these hands.
I am nobody; I have nothing to do with explosions.
I have given my name and my day-clothes up to the nurses
And my history to the anesthetist and my body to surgeons.

They have propped my head between the pillow and the sheet-cuff
Like an eye between two white lids that will not shut.
Stupid pupil, it has to take everything in.
The nurses pass and pass, they are no trouble,
They pass the way gulls pass inland in their white caps,
Doing things with their hands, one just the same as another,
So it is impossible to tell how many there are.

My body is a pebble to them, they tend it as water
Tends to the pebbles it must run over, smoothing them gently.
They bring me numbness in their bright needles, they bring me sleep.
Now I have lost myself I am sick of baggage ——
My patent leather overnight case like a black pillbox,
My husband and child smiling out of the family photo;
Their smiles catch onto my skin, little smiling hooks.

I have let things slip, a thirty-year-old cargo boat
Stubbornly hanging on to my name and address.
They have swabbed me clear of my loving associations.
Scared and bare on the green plastic-pillowed trolley
I watched my teaset, my bureaus of linen, my books
Sink out of sight, and the water went over my head.
I am a nun now, I have never been so pure.

I didn't want any flowers, I only wanted
To lie with my hands turned up and be utterly empty.
How free it is, you have no idea how free ——
The peacefulness is so big it dazes you,
And it asks nothing, a name tag, a few trinkets.

It is what the dead close on, finally; I imagine them
Shutting their mouths on it, like a Communion tablet.

The tulips are too red in the first place, they hurt me.
Even through the gift paper I could hear them breathe
Lightly, through their white swaddlings, like an awful baby.
Their redness talks to my wound, it corresponds.
They are subtle: they seem to float, though they weigh me
down,
Upsetting me with their sudden tongues and their color,
A dozen red lead sinkers round my neck.

Nobody watched me before, now I am watched.
The tulips turn to me, and the window behind me
Where once a day the light slowly widens and slowly thins,
And I see myself, flat, ridiculous, a cut-paper shadow
Between the eye of the sun and the eyes of the tulips,
And I have no face, I have wanted to efface myself.
The vivid tulips eat my oxygen.

Before they came the air was calm enough,
Coming and going, breath by breath, without any fuss.
Then the tulips filled it up like a loud noise.
Now the air snags and eddies round them the way a river
Snags and eddies round a sunken rust-red engine.
They concentrate my attention, that was happy
Playing and resting without committing itself.

The walls, also, seem to be warming themselves.
The tulips should be behind bars like dangerous animals;
They are opening like the mouth of some great African cat,
And I am aware of my heart: it opens and closes
Its bowl of red blooms out of sheer love of me.
The water I taste is warm and salt, like the sea,
And comes from a country far away as health.

(1961, *1965*)

Vicki Feaver

White Tulips

Last night I saw you in my dream:
wrenching the hands off clocks,
tearing out springs, weights, jewels.
And now I find you in an orchard,
lying face-up under red blossom
like one of those stone kings
with lion cubs at their feet.
There's a smile on your face;
you're surrounded by white tulips.
You must have cored the earth,
pushed home the papery bulbs
just for this moment — knowing
I'd peer through locked gates,
pressing my forehead against
a blacksmith's tracery
of bells and whorled leaves.
I feel myself shrinking, drying —
skin, bones, nerves, veins
contracting. I fly into the white bowls
of the flowers, emerge sticky with nectar
and pollen, alight on your neck, crawl
under your shirt, and sting.

(*1994*)

Selima Hill

My Father's Tulips

What the smell of the smell of my girl-friend's boy-friend's
  jumper
does to my dreams
is nobody's business but mine,

nor the smell of my father
going upstairs with his tulips
and passing me by on my bed like a still-born lamb.

(*1998*)

Magnoliaceae: Magnolia family

Langston Hughes

Magnolia Flowers

The quiet fading out of life
In a corner full of ugliness.

I went lookin' for magnolia flowers
But I didn't find 'em.
I went lookin' for magnolia flowers in the dusk
And there was only this corner
Full of ugliness.

'Scuse me,
I didn't mean to stump ma toe on you, lady.

There ought to be magnolias
Somewhere in this dusk.

'Scuse me,
I didn't mean to stump ma toe on you.

(*1959*)

Magnolia spp.
magnolia

Himalayas to Japan and west Malaysia, eastern North America to tropical America

Malvaceae: Mallow family

August Kleinzahler

Hollyhocks in the Fog

Every evening smoke blows in from the sea,
vapor of lost destroyers.
It hangs over the eucalyptus grove,
blocks every height,
curls around garbage sacks
next to a lesbian bar.
A black dog takes a long sprint through it, stops
squats and runs on.
                                        Cold smoke
seeps into the bloodstream, cancelling
the high ground of memory and pain —
a kind of war drug.

Some small piece is lost each time the smoke
moves through.
There is a part will have slipped away
when the sun burns back the world.
Here is a specific chill we wrap
ourselves against nightly.

Only the hollyhocks contend anything,
indelible and bright —
beacons, trembling.

What are those? I asked a friend
my first summer.

Now I wait for them.

(*1985*)

Alcea rosea
hollyhock

Possible hybrid of *A. setosa* (Crete and Turkey) and *A. pallida* (central and south-east Europe)

Jean Toomer

November Cotton Flower

Boll-weevil's coming, and the winter's cold,
Made cotton-stalks look rusty, seasons old,
And cotton, scarce as any southern snow,
Was vanishing; the branch, so pinched and slow,
Failed in its function as the autumn rake;
Drouth fighting soil had caused the soil to take
All water from the streams; dead birds were found
In wells a hundred feet below the ground —
Such was the season when the flower bloomed.
Old folks were startled, and it soon assumed
Significance. Superstition saw
Something it had never seen before:
Brown eyes that loved without a trace of fear,
Beauty so sudden for that time of year.

(*1923*)

Gossypium barbadense
Sea Island cotton

Widely planted in the southern United States; of South American origin, transported to the Caribbean, then to coastal Southern Carolina and Georgia

'The early forms of cotton cultivated in Asia, which were first spun in India, most likely came from a wild tree native to Africa. Geneticists have established that the presence of wild and cultivated cotton in the pre-Columbian Americas is due to a very early flotation of seed across the oceans, rather than human contact.' (Toby and Will Musgrave, *An Empire of Plants*, p.65)

Myoporaceae: Ngaio-Tree family

James K. Baxter

The Ngaio Tree

What happened under the low
green tarred ngaio branch cannot
be clearly remembered, but
determined what we know now,

ache of limit, an idyll
interrupted by thunder
heard by dead people who were
bowed each one under evil,

who knew the south gale blowing
spray on crops, or a woman
upright framed in her coffin
by foreseeing. No such thing

weighs on us, but just now the
feel of a strait-jacket, this
hard loop, dry sack of canvas,
as limbs touch, under the tree.

(1964, *1974*)

Myoporum laetum
ngaio tree

New Zealand

Myrtaceae: Myrtle family

Les Murray

Angophora floribunda

That country seemed one great park
in which stood big bridal trees
raining nectar and white thread
as native things ate their blossom
like hills of wheaten bread
and we called them Apple trees
our homesickness being sore
if you took up land where they grew
it kept your descendants half poor . . .

but farmers rarely cut them down.
They survive from the Eden of the country
because the wood's useless and rots fast
and because they're the Eden of the country.

Slashed leaves feed stock in a drought
and the tree, in its dirt-coloured bark
and snakes-and-laddery branchage
often grows aslant, heeled over
like an apple-pie schooner aground
on the shores of a North Coast pig farm.

Aged ones get cancerous
with humps of termite nest.
They shed their rotted limbs
to lie around them like junk
which only decay can burn.
A chewed-paper termite city
set alight in an Apple trunk
will rage all night and never
ignite its crucible of wood.

A veteran may drop most of itself
in one crash autumn, and re-grow from its boot.
Uselessness, sprawl and resurrection
are this apple's fruit.

(*2001*)

Angophora floribunda
gum myrtles, 'apples' (in Australia)

East Australia

Les Murray

Flowering Eucalypt in Autumn

That slim creek out of the sky
the dried-blood western gum-tree
is all stir in its high reaches:

its strung haze-blue foliage is dancing
points down in breezy mobs, swapping
pace and place in an all-over sway

retarded en masse by crimson blossom.
Bees still at work up there tack
around their exploded furry likeness

and the lawn underneath's a napped rug
of eyelash drift, of blooms flared
like a sneeze in a redhaired nostril,

minute urns, pinch-sized rockets
knocked down by winds, by night-creaking
fig-squirting bats, or the daily

parrot gang with green pocketknife wings.
Bristling food for tough delicate
raucous life, each flower comes

as a spray in its own turned vase,
a taut starburst, honeyed model
of the tree's fragrance crisping in your head.

When the Japanese plum tree
was shedding in spring, we speculated
there among the drizzling petals

what kind of exquisitely precious
artistic bloom might be gendered
in a pure ethereal compost

of petals potted as they fell.
From unpetalled gum-debris
we know what is grown continually,

a tower of fabulous swish tatters,
a map hoisted upright, a crusted
riverbed with up-country show towns.

(*1983*)

Eucalyptus spp.
eucalyptus, gum tree

Australia and east Malaysia (a few species only)

Oodgeroo Noonuccal (Kath Walker)

Municipal Gum

Gumtree in the city street,
Hard bitumen around your feet,
Rather you should be
In the cool world of leafy forest halls
And wild bird calls.
Here you seem to me
Like that poor cart-horse
Castrated, broken, a thing wronged,
Strapped and buckled, its hell prolonged,
Whose hung head and listless mien express
Its hopelessness.
Municipal gum, it is dolorous
To see you thus
Set in your black grass of bitumen —
O fellow citizen,
What have they done to us?

(*1966*)

Nelumbonaceae: Lotus family

Les Murray

Lotus Dam

Lotus leaves, standing feet above the water,
collect at their centre a perfect lens of rain
and heel, and tip it back into the water.

Their baby leaves are feet again, or slant lips
scrolled in declaration; pointed at toe and heel
they echo an unwalked sole in their pale green crinkles

and under blown and picket blooms, the floor
of floating leaves rolls light rainwater marbles
back and forth on sharkskins of anchored rippling.

Each speculum, pearl and pebble of the first water
rides, sprung with weight, on its live mirroring skin
tipped green and loganberry, till one or the other sky

redeems it, beneath bent foils and ferruled canes
where cupped pink bursts all day, above riddled water.

(*1987*)

Nelumbo spp.

Southern and eastern North America, West Indies to Columbia, Lower Volga, south and south-east Asia to tropical Australia

Toru Dutt

The Lotus

Love came to Flora asking for a flower
  That would of flowers be undisputed queen,
  The lily and the rose, long, long had been
Rivals for that high honour. Bards of power
Had sung their claims. 'The rose can never tower
  Like the pale lily with her Juno mien' —
  'But is the lily lovelier?' Thus between
Flower-factions rang the strife in Psyche's bower.
'Give me a flower delicious as the rose
  And stately as the lily in her pride' —
'But of what colour?' — 'Rose-red', Love first chose,
  Then prayed, — 'No, lily-white, — or, both provide';
  And Flora gave the lotus, 'rose-red' dyed,
And 'lily-white', queenliest flower that blows.

(*1882*)

Nelumbo speciosa
sacred lotus, Egyptian bean

South and South-East Asia to tropical Australia
Red flowers sacred in India, China and Tibet; in the Hindu religion considered to have sprung from the navel of the god Vishnu and to have given birth to Brahma, creator of the world; introduced to Egypt *c.* 500 BC, but no longer found in the Nile

Nymphaeaceae: Water-Lily family

John Clare

Water-Lilies

The water-lilies on the meadow stream
  Again spread out their leaves of glossy green;
And some, yet young, of a rich copper gleam,
  Scarce open, in the sunny stream are seen,
Throwing a richness upon Leisure's eye,
  That thither wanders in a vacant joy;
While on the sloping banks, luxuriantly,
  Tending of horse and cow, the chubby boy,
In self-delighted whims, will often throw
  Pebbles, to hit and splash their sunny leaves;
Yet quickly dry again, they shine and glow
  Like some rich vision that his eye deceives;
Spreading above the water, day by day,
In dangerous deeps, yet out of danger's way.

(1824–32, *1835*)

Nymphaea spp.
water-lily

Varied (and obscure) origins worldwide

William Barnes

The Clote

(*Water-Lily*)

O zummer clote! when the brook's a-glidèn
  So slow an' smooth down his zedgy bed,
Upon thy broad leaves so seäfe a-ridèn
  The water's top wi' thy yollow head,
    By alder's heads, O,
    An' bulrush beds, O,
Thou then dost float, goolden zummer clote!

The grey-bough'd withy's a-leänèn lowly
  Above the water thy leaves do hide;
The bendèn bulrush, a-swaÿèn slowly,
  Do skirt in zummer thy river's zide;
    An' perch in shoals, O,
    Do vill the holes, O,
Where thou dost float, goolden zummer clote!

Oh! when thy brook-drinkèn flow'r's a-blowèn,
  The burnèn zummer's a-zettèn in;
The time o' greenness, the time o' mowèn,
  When in the haÿ-vield, wi' zunburnt skin,
    The vo'k do drink, O,
    Upon the brink, O,
Where thou dost float, goolden zummer clote!

Wi' eärms a-spreadèn, an' cheäks a-blowèn,
  How proud wer I when I vu'st could zwim
Athirt the pleäce where thou bist a-growèn,
  Wi' thy long more vrom the bottom dim;
    While cows, knee-knigh, O,
    In brook, wer nigh, O,
Where thou dost float, goolden zummer clote!

Ov all the brooks drough the meäds a-windèn,
  Ov all the meäds by a river's brim,
There's nwone so faëir o' my own heart's vindèn,
  As where the maïdens do zee thee zwim,

An’ stan’ to teäke, O,
Wi’ long-stemm’d reäke, O,
Thy flow’r afloat, goolden zummer clote!

(*1844*)

Isabella Valancy Crawford

The Lily Bed

His cedar paddle, scented, red,
He thrust down through the lily bed;

Cloaked in a golden pause he lay,
Locked in the arms of the placid bay.

Trembled alone his bark canoe
As shocks of bursting lilies flew

Thro' the still crystal of the tide,
And smote the frail boat's birchen side;

Or, when besides the sedges thin
Rose the sharp silver of a fin;

Or when, a wizard swift and cold,
A dragon-fly beat out in gold

And jewels all the widening rings
Of waters singing to his wings;

Or, like a winged and burning soul,
Dropped from the gloom an oriole

On the cool wave, as to the balm
Of the Great Spirit's open palm

The freed soul flies. And silence clung
To the still hours, as tendrils hung,

In darkness carven, from the trees,
Sedge-buried to their burly knees.

Stillness sat in his lodge of leaves;
Clung golden shadows to its eaves,

And on its cone-spiced floor, like maize,
Red-ripe, fell sheaves of knotted rays.

The wood, a proud and crested brave;
Bead-bright, a maiden, stood the wave.

And he had spoke his soul of love
With voice of eagle and of dove.

Of loud, strong pines his tongue was made;
His lips, soft blossoms in the shade,

That kissed her silver lips — her's cool
As lilies on his inmost pool —

Till now he stood, in triumph's rest,
His image painted in her breast.

One isle 'tween blue and blue did melt, —
A bead of wampum from the belt

Of Manitou — a purple rise
On the far shore heaved to the skies.

His cedar paddle, scented, red,
He drew up from the lily bed;

All lily-locked, all lily-locked,
His light bark in the blossoms rocked.

Their cool lips round the sharp prow sang,
Their soft clasp to the frail sides sprang,

With breast and lip they wove a bar.
Stole from her lodge the Evening Star;

With golden hand she grasped the mane
Of a red cloud on her azure plain.

It by the peaked, red sunset flew;
Cool winds from its bright nostrils blew.

They swayed the high, dark trees, and low
Swept the locked lilies to and fro.

With cedar paddle, scented, red,
He pushed out from the lily bed.

(*1880*, *1905*)

Oleaceae: Olive family

Chris Wallace-Crabbe

Jasmine

A presence — how can you name a smell? —
heavy, hazed, like peaches and honey perhaps,
spreading over the lawns and lanes;

look to the flowers, dense on their dark-green
pointed leaves and upcurving tendrils.
They are fivefold stars of white,

they have crooked points, they are
spokes of a series of wheels turning clockwise,
there is a touch of yellow inside the corolla.

Sweetness of jasmine,
it bends up from the rickety paling fence
by untended beans and caulies.

Can such floods
of scent
come from those frail starfish
bunched high on the tennis-court wire?

The gravel swoons,
the lobs drop back.

(*1985*)

Jasminum officinale
jasmine

Caucasus to south-west China

Meena Alexander

Jasmine

Whichever way I move my palms
the pugnacious scents of jasmine
linger. They say it is a woman's
flower, this querulous hybrid
trained against the courtyard walls.

Blooms smother the key, rusty
with disuse (her grandfather's
father melted down the lock).
The vehement groom remembers
a worn horsewhip, ashen gloom.

(*1980*)

Alice Fulton

Forcing White Lilacs

First   the cold
the being held
to the ground.
Then to see things
the police won't
use, how his eyes
are tortoise shell, cracked
shoes layered with blacking,
the cigar and sweat smell
in the clothes   he rips
while snow drives
into her skin.
Her fear flaps at him
like a bat's shrieks
rebounding from trees
and she already dreads
the time it will take
to forget   the deep wavy tread
in his hair.
He is a squeezed tube
spurting words that knife
and twine like eels
under ice. He is all flesh
that wants into
hers. She forces herself
to think of anything
else: the flakes
a veil of buds   above
his shoulder she can see
light years of stars
yet night has knit
a stocking for his face.
He could be anyone
in the mild scum
of moon   he leaves
a foam on her jeans
she thinks of white
lilacs white lilacs

the first time   thighs
like packed snow
a sibilance of pigeons:
her cries unwinding
from his ears.

(*1979*)

Syringa hybrid
white lilac

Garden origin

Onagraceae: Willowherb family

Amy Clampitt

Fireweed

A single seedling, camp-follower
of arson — frothing bombed-out
rubble with rose-purple lotfuls

unwittingly as water overbrims,
tarn-dark or sun-ignited, down
churnmilk rockfalls — aspiring

from the foothold of a London
roof-ledge, taken wistful note of
by an uprooted prairie-dweller,

less settled in St Martin's Lane
(no lane now but a riverbed of
noise) than even the unlikely

blackbird that's to be heard here,
gilding and regilding a matutinal
ancestral scripture, unwitting

of past devastation as of what
remains: spires, finials, lofted
domes, the homiletic caveat

underneath — *Here wee have no
continuing citty* — by the Dean
whose effigy survived one burning.

(*1991*)

Epilobium angustifolium
rosebay willowherb, wickup

Northern temperate regions worldwide

Thomas Hardy

The Lodging-House Fuchsias

Mrs Masters's fuchsias hung
Higher and broader, and brightly swung,
    Bell-like, more and more
Over the narrow garden-path,
Giving the passer a sprinkle-bath
        In the morning.

She put up with their pushful ways
And made us tenderly lift their sprays,
    Going to her door:
But when her funeral had to pass
They cut back all the flowery mass
        In the morning.

(*1928*)

Fuchsia spp.
fuchsia

Central and South America, Tahiti, New Zealand

John Clare

Evening Primrose

When once the sun sinks in the west,
And dew-drops pearl the Evening's breast;
Almost as pale as moonbeams are,
Or its companionable star,
The Evening Primrose opes anew
Its delicate blossoms to the dew;
And hermit-like, shunning the light,
Wastes its fair bloom upon the Night;
Who, blindfold to its fond caresses,
Knows not the beauty he possesses.
Thus it blooms on while Night is by;
When Day looks out with open eye,
'Bashed at the gaze it cannot shun,
It faints, and withers, and is gone.

(1821–4, *1835*)

Oenothera biennis
evening primrose

Europe

Orchidaceae: Orchid family

Theodore Roethke

Orchids

They lean over the path,
Adder-mouthed,
Swaying close to the face,
Coming out, soft and deceptive,
Limp and damp, delicate as a young bird's tongue;
Their fluttery fledgling lips
Move slowly,
Drawing in the warm air.

And at night,
The faint moon falling through whitewashed glass,
The heat going down
So their musky smell comes even stronger,
Drifting down from their mossy cradles:
So many devouring infants!
Soft luminescent fingers,
Lips neither dead nor alive,
Loose ghostly mouths
Breathing.

(*1948*)

Orchidaceae spp.
orchid

Cosmopolitan

Medbh McGuckian

The Orchid House

A flower's fragrance is a woman's virtue;
So I tell them underground in pairs,
Or in their fleshy white sleeves, how
Desirable their shapes, how one
Was lost for sixty years, with all
Its arching spikes, its honeyed tessellations,
And how in bloom they will resemble
Moths, the gloss of mirrors, Christmas
Stars, their helmets blushing
Red-brown when they marry.

(*1982*)

Jackie Kay

Keeping Orchids

The orchids my mother gave me when we first met
are still alive, twelve days later. Although

some of the buds remain closed as secrets.
Twice since I carried them back, like a baby in a shawl,

from her train station to mine, then home. Twice
since then the whole glass carafe has crashed

falling over, unprovoked, soaking my chest of drawers.
All the broken waters. I have rearranged

the upset orchids with troubled hands. Even after
that the closed ones did not open out. The skin

shut like an eye in the dark; the closed lid.
Twelve days later, my mother's hands are all I have.

Her face is fading fast. Even her voice rushes
through a tunnel the other way from home.

I close my eyes and try to remember exactly:
a paisley pattern scarf, a brooch, a navy coat.

A digital watch her daughter was wearing when she died.
Now they hang their heads,

and suddenly grow old — the proof of meeting. Still,
her hands, awkward and hard to hold

fold and unfold a green carrier bag as she tells
the story of her life. Compressed. Airtight.

A sad square, then a crumpled shape. A bag of tricks.
Her secret life — a hidden album, a box of love letters.

A door opens and closes. Time is outside waiting.
I catch the draught in my winter room.

Airlocks keep the cold air out.
Boiling water makes flowers live longer. So does
cutting the stems with a sharp knife.

(*1993*)

Mary Oliver

Moccasin Flowers

All my life,
  so far,
    I have loved
      more than one thing,

including the mossy hooves
  of dreams, including
    the spongy litter
      under the tall trees.

In spring
  the moccasin flowers
    reach for the crackling
      lick of the sun

and burn down. Sometimes,
  in the shadows,
    I see the hazy eyes,
      the lamb-lips

of oblivion,
  its deep drowse,
    and I can imagine a new nothing
      in the universe,

the matted leaves splitting
  open, revealing
    the black planks
      of the stairs.

But all my life — so far —
  I have loved best
    how the flowers rise
      and open, how

the pink lungs of their bodies
  enter the fire of the world
    and stand there shining
      and willing — the one

thing they can do before
they shuffle forward
into the floor of darkness, they
become the trees.

(*1990*)

Cypripedium spp.
lady's-slipper orchids

Northern temperate regions
Protected in the UK, though allegedly reduced to a single flower in Yorkshire through over-collection

Michael Longley

The Ghost Orchid

Added to its few remaining sites will be the stanza
I compose about leaves like flakes of skin, a colour
Dithering between pink and yellow, and then the root
That grows like coral among shadows and leaf-litter.
Just touching the petals bruises them into darkness.

(*1995*)

Epipogium aphyllum
ghost orchid

Old-World tropics to Australia

Judith Wright

Phaius Orchid

Out of the brackish sand
see the phaius orchid build
her intricate moonlight tower
that rusts away in flower.

For whose eyes — for whose eyes
does this blind being weave
sand's poverty, water's sour,
the white and black of the hour

into the image I hold
and cannot understand?
Is it for the ants, the bees,
the lizard outside his cave,

or is it to garland time —
eternity's cold tool
that severs with its blade
the gift as soon as made?

Then I too am your fool.
What can I do but believe?
Here like the plant I weave
your dying garlands, time.

(*1953*)

Phaius spp.
phaius orchid

Indo-Malaysia to south China, tropical Africa and Australia, New Caledonia

Paeoniaceae: Paeony family

Jane Kenyon

Peonies at Dusk

White peonies blooming along the porch
send out light
while the rest of the yard grows dim.

Outrageous flowers as big as human
heads! They're staggered
by their own luxuriance: I had
to prop them up with stakes and twine.

The moist air intensifies their scent,
and the moon moves around the barn
to find out what it's coming from.

In the darkening June evening
I draw a blossom near, and bending close
search it as a woman searches
a loved one's face.

(*1996*)

Paeonia spp. or hybrids
paeony

Temperate Eurasia, western North America

Palmae: Palm family

W. S. Merwin

The Palms

Each is alone in the world
and on some the flowers
are of one sex only

they stand as though they had no secrets
and one by one the flowers emerge from the sheaths
into the air
where the other flowers are
it happens in silence except for the wind
often it happens in the dark
with the earth carrying the sound of water

most of the flowers themselves are small and green by day
and only a few are fragrant
but in time the fruits are beautiful
and later still their children
whether they are seen or not

many of the fruits are no larger than peas
but some are like brains of black marble
and some have more than one seed inside them
some are full of milk of one taste or another
and on a number of them there is a writing
from long before speech

and the children resemble each other
with the same family preference
for shade when young
in which their colors deepen
and the same family liking for water
and warmth
and each family deals with the wind in its own way
and with the sun and the water

some of the leaves are crystals others are stars
some are bows some are bridges and some
are hands
in a world without hands

they know of each other first from themselves
some are fond of limestone and a few cling to high cliffs
they learn from the splashing water
and the falling water and the wind

much later the elephant
will learn from them
the muscles will learn from their shadows
ears will begin to hear in them
the sound of water
and heads will float like black nutshells
on an unmeasured ocean neither rising nor falling

to be held up at last and named for the sea

(*1993*)

Palmae spp.
palm

Tropics

Roy Campbell

The Palm

Blistered and dry was the desert I trod
When out of the sky with the step of a god,
Victory-vanned, with her feathers out-fanned,
The palm tree alighting my journey delayed
And spread me, inviting, her carpet of shade.
Vain were evasions, though urgent my quest,
And there as the guest of her rustling persuasions
To lie in the shade of her branches was best.
Like a fountain she played, spilling plume over plume in
A leafy cascade for the winds to illumine,
Ascending in brilliance and falling in shade,
And spurning the ground with a tiptoe resilience,
Danced to the sound of the music she made.
Her voice intervened on my shadowed seclusion
Like a whispered intrusion of seraph or fiend,
In its tone was the hiss of the serpent's wise tongue
But soft as the kiss of a lover it stung —
'Unstrung is your lute? For despair are you silent?
Am I not an island in oceans as mute?
Around me the thorns of the desert take root;
Though I spring from the rock of a region accurst,
Yet fair is the daughter of hunger and thirst
Who sings like the water the valleys have nursed,
And rings her blue shadow as deep and as cool
As the heavens of azure that sleep on a pool.
And you, who so soon by the toil were undone,
Could you guess through what horrors my beauty had won
Ere I crested the noon as the bride of the sun?
The roots are my anchor struck fast in the hill,
The higher I hanker, the deeper they drill,
Through the red mortar their claws interlock
To ferret the water through warrens of rock.
Each inch of my glory was wrenched with a groan,
Corroded with fire from the base of my throne
And drawn like a wire from the heart of a stone:
Though I soar in the height with the shape of delight
Uplifting my stem like the string of a kite,
Yet still must each grade of my climbing be told

And still from the summit my measure I hold,
Sounding the azure with plummet of gold.
Partaking the strain of the heavenward pride
That soars me away from the earth I deride,
Though my stem be a rein that would tether me down
And fasten a chain on the height of my crown,
Yet through its tense nerve do I measure my might,
The strain of its curb is the strength of my flight:
And when, by the hate of the hurricane blown,
It doubles its forces with fibres that groan,
Exulting I ride in the tower of my pride
To feel that the strength of the blast is my own . . .
Rest under my branches, breathe deep of my balm
From the hushed avalanches of fragrance and calm,
For suave is the silence that poises the palm.
The wings of the egrets are silken and fine,
But hushed with the secrets of Eden are mine:
Your spirit that grieves like the wind in my leaves
Shall be robbed of its care by those whispering thieves
To study my patience and hear, the day long,
The soft foliations of sand into song —
For bitter and cold though it rasp to my root,
Each atom of gold is the chance of a fruit,
The sap is the music, the stem is the flute,
And the leaves are the wings of the seraph I shape
Who dances, who springs in a golden escape,
Out of the dust and the drought of the plain,
To sing with the silver hosannas of rain'.

(*1930*)

John Agard

Palm Tree King

Because I come from the West Indies
certain people in England seem to think
I is a expert on palm trees

So not wanting to sever dis link
with me native roots (know what ah mean?)
or to disappoint dese culture vulture
I does smile cool as seabreeze

and say to dem
which specimen
you interested in
cause you talking
to the right man
I is palm tree king
I know palm tree history
like de palm o me hand
In fact me navel string
bury under a palm tree

If you think de queen could wave
you ain't see nothing yet
till you see the Roystonea Regia
— that is the royal palm —
with she crown of leaves
waving calm-calm
over the blue Caribbean carpet
nearly 100 feet of royal highness

But let we get down to business
Tell me what you want to know
How tall a palm tree does grow?
What is the biggest coconut I ever see?
What is the average length of the leaf?

Don't expect me to be brief
cause palm tree history
is a long-long story

Anyway why you so interested
in length and circumference?

That kind of talk so ordinary
That don't touch the essence
of palm tree mystery
That is no challenge
to a palm tree historian like me

Is you insist on statistics
why you don't pose a question
with some mathematical profundity?

Ask me something more tricky
like if a American tourist with a camera
take 9 minutes to climb a coconut tree
how long a English tourist without a camera
would take to climb the same coconut tree?

That is problem pardner
Now ah coming harder

If 6 straw hat
and half a dozen bikini
multiply by the same number of coconut tree
equal one postcard
how many square miles of straw hat
you need to make a tourist industry?

That is problem pardner
Find the solution
and you got a revolution

But before you say anything
let I palm tree king
give you dis warning
Ah want de answer in metric
it kind of rhyme with tropic
Besides it sound more exotic

(*1983*)

Hart Crane

Royal Palm

For Grace Hart Crane

Green rustlings, more-than-regal charities
Drift coolly from that tower of whispered light.
Amid the noontide's blazed asperities
I watched the sun's most gracious anchorite

Climb up as by communings, year on year
Uneaten of the earth or aught earth holds,
And the grey trunk, that's elephantine, rear
Its frondings sighing in aetherial folds.

Forever fruitless, and beyond that yield
Of sweat the jungle presses with hot love
And tendril till our deathward breath is sealed —
It grazes the horizons, launched above

Mortality — ascending, emerald-bright,
A fountain at salute, a crown in view —
Unshackled, casual of its azured height
As though it soared suchwise through heaven too.

(*1927*)

Roystonea regia
royal palm

Cuba and Florida, United States

Papaveraceae: Poppy family

Ted Hughes

Big Poppy

Hot-eyed Mafia Queen!
At the trim garden's edge

She sways towards August.
A Bumble Bee
Clambers into her drunken, fractured goblet —

Up the royal carpet of a down-hung,
Shrivel-edged, unhinged petal, her first-about-to-fall.
He's in there as she sways. He utters thin

Sizzling bleats of difficult enjoyment.
Her carnival paper skirts, luminous near-orange,
Embrace him helplessly.

Already her dark pod is cooking its drug.
Every breath imperils her. Her crucible
Is falling apart with its own fierceness.

A fly, cool, rests on the flame-fringe.

Soon she'll throw off her skirts
Withering into vestal afterlife,

Bleeding inwardly
Her maternal nectars into her own
Coffin — (cradle of her offspring).

Then we shall say:
'She wore herself in her hair, in her day,
And we could see nothing but her huge flop of petal,

Her big, lewd, bold eye, in its sooty lashes,

And that stripped, athletic leg, hairy,
In a fling of abandon —'

(*1986*)

Papaver orientale
poppy

Europe, Asia, Cape Verde Islands, southern Africa, western North America; probably introduced to Australia

Anna Seward

Sonnet. To the Poppy

While summer roses all their glory yield
  To crown the votary of love and joy,
  Misfortune's victim hails, with many a sigh,
  Thee, scarlet Poppy of the pathless field,
Gaudy, yet wild and lone; no leaf to shield
  Thy flaccid vest that, as the gale blows high,
  Flaps, and alternate folds around thy head.
  So stands in the long grass a love-crazed maid,
Smiling aghast; while stream to every wind
  Her garish ribbons, smeared with dust and rain;
  But brain-sick visions cheat her tortured mind,
And bring false peace. Thus, lulling grief and pain,
  Kind dreams oblivious from thy juice proceed,
  Thou flimsy, showy, melancholy weed.

(*c.* 1789; *1799*)

August Kleinzahler

Poppies in the Wind

The honeybee
painting himself his delight inside her
the both of them
adrift
tossing in fits of wind
petals of her knees
raised up around him
petal arms
encircling in shadow his cameo'd frenzy
hosts of them
open or clenched
waving
sheathed or half out
of their witch-hats
at May's meridian
drying like chicks in the air

(*1985*)

Sylvia Plath

Poppies in July

Little poppies, little hell flames,
Do you do no harm?

You flicker. I cannot touch you.
I put my hands among the flames. Nothing burns.

And it exhausts me to watch you
Flickering like that, wrinkly and clear red, like the skin of a
mouth.

A mouth just bloodied.
Little bloody skirts!

There are fumes that I cannot touch.
Where are your opiates, your nauseous capsules?

If I could bleed or sleep! —
If my mouth could marry a hurt like that!

Or your liquors seep to me, in this glass capsule,
Dulling and stilling.

But colorless. Colorless.

(1962, *1965*)

Sylvia Plath

Poppies in October

Even the sun-clouds this morning cannot manage such skirts.
Nor the woman in the ambulance
Whose red heart blooms through her coat so astoundingly ——

A gift, a love gift
Utterly unasked for
By a sky

Palely and flamily
Igniting its carbon monoxides, by eyes
Dulled to a halt under bowlers.

O my God, what am I
That these late mouths should cry open
In a forest of frost, in a dawn of cornflowers.

(1962, *1965*)

Michael Longley

Poppies

I

Some people tried to stop other people wearing poppies
And ripped them from lapels as though uprooting poppies
From Flanders fields, but the others hid inside their poppies
Razor blades and added to their poppies more red poppies.

II

In Royal Avenue they tossed in the air with so much joy
Returning wounded soldiers, their stitches burst for joy.

(*1995*)

Phytolaccaceae: Pokeweed family

Amy Clampitt

Vacant Lot with Pokeweed

Tufts, follicles, grubstake
biennial rosettes, a low-
life beach-blond scruff of
couch grass: notwithstanding
the interglinting dregs

of wholesale upheaval and
dismemberment, weeds do not
hesitate, the wheeling
rise of the ailanthus halts
at nothing — and look! here's

a pokeweed, sprung from seed
dropped by some vagrant, that's
seized a foothold: a magenta-
girdered bower, gazebo twirls
of blossom rounding into

raw-buttoned, garnet-rodded
fruit one more wayfarer
perhaps may salvage from
the season's frittering,
the annual wreckage.

(*1991*)

Phytolacca americana
pokeweed, pigeonberry, inkberry

North America

Pinaceae: Pine family

Ruth Pitter

The Cedar

Look from the high window with the eye of wonder
When the sun soars over and the moon dips under.

Look when the sun is coming and the moon is going
On the aspiring creature, on the cedar growing.

Plant or world? are those lights and shadows
Branches, or great air-suspended meadows?

Boles and branches, haunted by the flitting linnet,
Or great hillsides rolling up to cliffs or granite?

Those domed shapes, thick-clustered on the ledges,
Upright fruit, or dwellings thatched with sedges?

Fair through the eye of innocence returning,
This is a country hanging in the morning;

Scented alps, where nothing but the daylight changes,
Climbing to black walls of mountain ranges;

And under the black walls, under the sky-banners,
The dwellings of the blessed in the green savannahs.

(*1953*)

Cedrus spp.
cedar

Mountains of North Africa to Asia

Hartley Coleridge

The Larch Grove

Line above line the nursling larches planted,
  Still as they climb with interspace more wide,
Let in and out the sunny beams that slanted,
  And shot and crankled down the mountain's side.

The larches grew, and darker grew the shade;
  And sweeter aye the fragrance of the Spring;
Pink pencils all the spiky boughs arrayed,
  And small green needles called the birds to sing.

They grew apace as fast as they could grow,
  As fain the tawny fell to deck and cover,
They haply thought to soothe the pensive woe,
  Or hide the joy of stealthy tripping lover.

Ah, larches! that shall never be your lot;
  Nought shall you have to do with amorous weepers,
Nor shall ye prop the roof of cozy cot,
  But rumble out your days as railway sleepers.

(*1851*)

Larix spp. or hybrid
larch

Cool northern hemisphere, Europe

Emily Dickinson

'I Think the Hemlock Likes to Stand' [525]

I think the Hemlock likes to stand
Upon a Marge of Snow —
It suits his own Austerity —
And satisfies an awe

That men, must slake in Wilderness —
And in the Desert — cloy —
An instinct for the Hoar, the Bald —
Lapland's — necessity —

The Hemlock's nature thrives — on cold —
The Gnash of Northern winds
Is sweetest nutriment — to him —
His best Norwegian Wines —

To satin Races — he is nought —
But children on the Don,
Beneath his Tabernacles, play,
And Dnieper Wrestlers, run.

(*c.* 1862, *1890*)

Tsuga spp.
hemlock (spruce)

Temperate North America and east Asia south to Vietnam

Platanaceae: Plane family

Roy Campbell

Autumn Plane

Peeled white and washed with fallen rain,
A dancer weighed with jingling pearls,
The girl-white body of a plane,
In whose red hair the Autumn swirls,
Stands out, soliciting the cruel
Flame of the wintry sun, and dies,
If only to the watcher's eyes,
In red-gold anguish glowing; fuel
To that cold fire, as she assumes
(Brunhilde) her refulgent plumes
In leaves that kindle as they die,
Of all that triumphs and returns
The furious aurora burns
Against the winter-boding sky.

(*1933*)

Platanus spp.
plane

Northern hemisphere, South-East Asia

Polemoniaceae: Phlox family

Sandra McPherson

Phlox Diffusa

A Poem for My Fiftieth Birthday

Is it calm after midnight on its rocky slope,
exactly fitted to its nice little rubble?
Easy to think it's a bedtime slipper of a flower, owning no boots.
It lies flat on its back and looks at stars.

'Undaunted by stern surroundings', Mary Elizabeth Parson says
in *Wild Flowers of California*, 1907.
Like the game pummeled seapalm on outer rocks in breakers
the phlox spreads happy in its xeric meadow.

The flowers completely hide the leaf cushion,
the way a lot of enthusiasms obscure
the inner idiot. Actually clothe it,
but wildly as a shopping spree.

Charmed and usually older hikers want to lie right down beside it.
Starlike, delicate.

'The tiny crammed leaves live in a pocket of calm partly
of their own making, and there they trap
windblown particles
that slowly become a nourishing soil.'

Taproots eight to fifteen feet.
A throw pillow bolted to granite.
Easy to think it's only three inches tall,
until you think of that, think of that root.

(*1996*)

Phlox diffusa
phlox

California, United States

Polygonaceae: Dock family

John Burnside

Russian Vine

This is what Spencer means when he paints
those gardens where a resurrection waits
to happen: coltsfoot and privet
etched with a glimmer of ink
                                        or a back lane
seeping away to reed and the dank retreats
of frog-eating birds

and why we planted it beyond the shed
to spill through the fence
and lope through the neighbour's yard
was closer to revenge against
his tight, edged lawns and rows of bedding plants
than human error: that there ought to be
a wildness in the world
                                that folk should dream
of mudslips and banks of spawn and sudden eyes
amongst the green
                            to mock this gendering.

(*2000*)

Fallopia aubertii
Russian vine

West China and Tibet

Primulaceae: Primrose family

'Michael Field'
(Katherine Harris Bradley and Edith Emma Cooper)

Cyclamens

    They are terribly white:
    There is snow on the ground,
  And a moon on the snow at night;
  The sky is cut by the winter light;
Yet I, who have all these things in ken,
Am struck to the heart by the chiselled white
  Of this handful of cyclamen.

(*1893*)

Cyclamen spp.
cyclamen

Europe, Mediterranean to Iran and north-east Somalia

Walter Savage Landor

To a Cyclamen

I come to visit thee again,
My little flowerless cyclamen!
To touch the hands, almost to press,
That cheer'd thee in thy loneliness.
What could those lovely sisters find,
Of thee in form, of me in mind,
What is there in us rich or rare,
To make us worth a moment's care?
Unworthy to be so carest,
We are but wither'd leaves at best.

(*1846*)

R. S. Thomas

Cyclamen

They are white moths
With wings
Lifted
Over a dark water
In act to fly,
Yet stayed
By their frail images
In its mahogany depths.

(*1946*)

John Clare

The Primrose

Welcome, pale Primrose! starting up between
  Dead matted leaves of ash and oak, that strew
  The every lawn, the wood, and spinney through,
Mid creeping moss and ivy's darker green;
  How much thy presence beautifies the ground:
How sweet thy modest, unaffected pride
Glows on the sunny bank, and wood's warm side.
  And when thy fairy flowers in groups are found,
The school-boy roams enchantedly along,
  Plucking the fairest with a rude delight:
While the meek shepherd stops his simple song,
  To gaze a moment on the pleasing sight;
O'erjoy'd to see the flowers that truly bring
The welcome news of sweet returning Spring.

(1809–19, *1820*)

Primula vulgaris
primrose

Europe

Robert Herrick

The Primrose

Aske me why I send you here
This sweet *Infanta* of the yeere?
Aske me why I send to you
This Primrose, thus bepearl'd with dew?
I will whisper to your eares,
The sweets of Love are mixt with tears.

2. Aske me why this flower do's show
So yellow-green, and sickly too?
Aske me why the stalk is weak
And bending, (yet it doth not break?)
I will answer, These discover
What fainting hopes are in a Lover.

(*1648*)

John Donne

The Primrose

Upon this Primrose hill,
Where, if Heav'n would distill
A shoure of raine, each severall drop might goe
To his owne primrose, and grow Manna so;
And where their forme, and their infinitie
Make a terrestriall Galaxie,
As the small starres doe in the skie:
I walke to finde a true Love; and I see
That 'tis not a mere woman, that is shee,
But must, or more, or lesse then woman bee.

Yet I know not, which flower
I wish; a sixe, or foure;
For should my true-Love lesse then woman bee,
She were scarce any thing; and then, should she
Be more then woman, shee would get above
All thought of sexe, and thinke to move
My heart to study her, not to love;
Both these were monsters; Since there must reside
Falshood in woman, I could more abide,
She were by art, then Nature falsify'd.

Live Primrose then, and thrive
With thy true number five;
And women, whom this flower doth represent,
With this mysterious number be content;
Ten is the farthest number, if halfe ten
Belongs unto each woman, then
Each woman may take halfe us men,
Or this will not serve their turne, Since all
Numbers are odde, or even, and they fall
First into this five, women may take us all.

(*1633*)

Ranunculaceae: Buttercup family

John Clare

Wood Anemone

The wood anemone through dead oak leaves
And in the thickest wood now blooms anew,
And where the green briar and the bramble weaves
Thick clumps of green, anemones thicker grew.
And weeping flowers in thousands pearled with dew
People the woods and brakes' hid hollows there
White, yellow, and purpled-hued the wide woods through:
What pretty, drooping weeping flowers they are!
The clipt-frilled leaves, the slender stalk they bear
On which the drooping flower hangs weeping dew!
How beautiful through April time and May
The woods look, filled with wild anemones!
And every little spinney now looks gay
With flowers mid brushwood and the huge oak trees.

(1842–64, *1935*)

Anemone nemorosa
wood anemone

Eurasia

Nora Hopper (later Chesson)

Marsh Marigolds

Here in the water-meadows
  Marsh marigolds ablaze
Brighten the elder shadows
  Lost in an autumn haze.
Drunkards of sun and summer
  They keep their colours clear,
Flaming among the marshes
  At waning of the year.

Thicker than bee-swung clovers
  They crowd the meadow-space;
Each to the mist that hovers
  Lifts an undaunted face.
Time, that has stripped the sunflower,
  And driven the bees away,
Hath on these golden gipsies
  No power to dismay.

Marsh marigolds together
  Their ragged banners lift
Against the darkening weather,
  Long rains and frozen drift:
They take the lessening sunshine
  Home to their hearts to keep
Against the days of darkness,
  Against the time of sleep.

(*1900*)

Caltha palustris
marsh marigold, kingcup, may blobs

Northern temperate regions

'The flower of *Caltha palustris* is perhaps the most "primitive" in the British flora.' (Clapham, Tutin and Warburg, *Flora of the British Isles*, p.58)

Emily Dickinson

'Tis Customary As We Part' [440]

'Tis customary as we part
A trinket — to confer
It helps to stimulate the faith
When Lovers be afar —

'Tis various — as the various taste —
Clematis — journeying far —
Presents me with a single Curl
Of her Electric Hair —

(*c.* 1862, *1945*)

Clematis spp.
clematis

Northern temperate regions, Europe, southern temperate regions, Oceania and tropical Africa

William Wordsworth

The Small Celandine

There is a Flower, the Lesser Celandine,
That shrinks, like many more, from cold and rain;
And, the first moment that the sun may shine,
Bright as the sun himself, 'tis out again!

When hailstones have been falling, swarm on swarm,
Or blasts the green field and the trees distrest,
Oft I have seen it muffled up from harm,
In close self-shelter, like a Thing at rest.

But lately, one rough day, this Flower I passed,
And recognized it, though an altered Form,
Now standing forth an offering to the Blast,
And buffeted at will by Rain and Storm.

I stopped, and said with inly muttered voice,
'It doth not love the shower, nor seek the cold:
This neither is its courage nor its choice,
But its necessity in being old.

'The sunshine may not cheer it, nor the dew;
It cannot help itself in its decay;
Stiff in its members, withered, changed of hue.'
And, in my spleen, I smiled that it was grey.

To be a Prodigal's Favorite — then, worse truth,
A Miser's Pensioner — behold our lot!
O Man! that from thy fair and shining youth
Age might but take the things Youth needed not!

(1803, *1807*)

Ranunculus ficaria
lesser celandine, pilewort

Europe, west Asia, naturalised in North America

Rosaceae: Rose family

Judith Wright

The Hawthorn Hedge

How long ago she planted the hawthorn hedge —
she forgets how long ago —
that barrier of thorn across the hungry ridge;
thorn and snow.

It is twice as tall as the rider on the tall mare
who draws his reins to peer
in through the bee-hung blossom. Let him stare.
No one is here.

Only the mad old girl from the hut on the hill,
unkempt as an old tree.
She will hide away if you wave your hand or call;
she will not see.

Year-long, wind turns her grindstone heart and whets
a thornbush like a knife,
shouting in winter 'Death'; and when the white bud sets,
more loudly, 'Life'.

She has forgotten when she planted the hawthorn hedge;
that thorn, that green, that snow;
birdsong and sun dazzled across the ridge —
it was long ago.

Her hands were strong in the earth, her glance on the sky,
her song was sweet on the wind.
The hawthorn hedge took root, grew wild and high
to hide behind.

(*1946*)

Crataegus monogyna
hawthorn, may

Europe

Seamus Heaney

The Haw Lantern

The wintry haw is burning out of season,
crab of the thorn, a small light for small people,
wanting no more from them but that they keep
the wick of self-respect from dying out,
not having to blind them with illumination.

But sometimes when your breath plumes in the frost
it takes the roaming shape of Diogenes
with his lantern, seeking just one man;
so you end up scrutinized from behind the haw
he holds up at eye-level on its twig,
and you flinch before its bonded pith and stone,
its blood-prick that you wish would test and clear you,
its pecked-at ripeness that scans you, then moves on.

(*1987*)

Anonymous

'Of Every Kinnë Tre'

Of every kinnë tre, *kind of*
Of every kinnë tre,
The hawthorn blowëth swetest, *blossoms sweetest*
Of every kinnë tre.

My lemman she shall be, *lover*
My lemman she shall be,
The fairest of every kinnë,
My lemman she shall be.

(*c.* 1325–50)
from *The Rawlinson Lyrics*

Kathleen Jamie

Meadowsweet

Tradition suggests that certain of the Gaelic women poets were buried face down

So they buried her, and turned home,
a drab psalm
hanging about them like haar,

not knowing the liquid
trickling from her lips
would seek its way down,

and that caught in her slowly
unravelling plait of grey hair
were summer seeds:

meadowsweet, bastard balm,
tokens of honesty, already
beginning their crawl

toward light, so showing her,
when the time came,
how to dig herself out —

to surface and greet them,
mouth young, and full again
of dirt, and spit, and poetry.

(*1999*)

Filipendula ulmaria
meadowsweet

Eurasia, naturalised in North America

Ruth Pitter

The Strawberry Plant

Above the water, in her rocky niche,
She sat enthroned and perfect; for her crown
One bud like pearl, and then two fairy roses
Blanched and yet ardent in their glowing hearts:
One greenish berry spangling into yellow
Where the light touched the seed: one fruit achieved
And ripe, an odorous vermilion ball
Tight with completion, lovingly enclasped
By the close cup whose green chimed with the red,
And showered with drops of gold like Danaë:
Three lovely sister leaves as like as peas,
Young but full-fledged, dark, with a little down:
Two leaves that to a matron hue inclined;
And one the matriarch, that dressed in gold
And flushed with wine, thought her last days her best.
And here and there a diamond of dew
Beamed coolly from the white, smiled from the gold,
Silvered the down, struck lightning for the red.
The overhanging rock forbade the sun,
Yet she was all alight with water-gleams
Reflected, like the footlights at a play:
Perfection's self, and (rightly) out of reach.

(*1936*)

Fragaria vesca
strawberry

Northern temperate regions

A. E. Housman

'Loveliest of Trees, the Cherry Now'

Loveliest of trees, the cherry now
Is hung with bloom along the bough,
And stands about the woodland ride
Wearing white for Eastertide.

Now, of my threescore years and ten,
Twenty will not come again,
And take from seventy springs a score,
It only leaves me fifty more.

And since to look at things in bloom
Fifty springs are little room,
About the woodlands I will go
To see the cherry hung with snow.

(*1896*)

Prunus avium
sweet cherry, gean, mazzard, hagberry

Eurasia

Edward Thomas

The Cherry Trees

The cherry trees bend over and are shedding,
On the road where all that passed are dead,
Their petals, strewing the grass as for a wedding
This early May morn when there is none to wed.

(*1917*)

Malcolm Lowry

The Wild Cherry

We put a prop beneath the sagging bough
That yearned over the beach, setting four stones
Cairn-like against it, but we thought our groans
Were the wild cherry's, for it was as though
Utterly set with broken seams on doom
It listed wilfully down like a mast,
Stubborn as some smashed recalcitrant boom
That will neither be cut loose nor made fast.
Going — going — it was yet no bidder
For life, whether for such sober healing
We left its dead branches to consider
Until its sunward pulse renewed, feeling
The passionate hatred of that tree
Whose longing was to wash away to sea.

(1940–7, *1962*, *1992*)

Thom Gunn

The Cherry Tree

In her gnarled sleep it
begins
        though she seems
as unmoving as the statue
of a running man: her
branches caught in a
writhing, her trunk
leaning as if in mid-fall.
When the wind moves
against her grave body
only the youngest twigs
scutter amongst themselves.

But there's something going on
in those twisted brown limbs,
it starts as a need
and it takes over, a need
to push
        push outward
from the center, to
bring what is not
from what is, pushing
till at the tips of the push
something comes about
                                        and then
pulling it from outside
until yes she has them started
tiny bumps
appear at the ends of twigs.

Then at once they're all here,
she wears them like a coat
a coat of babies,
I almost think that she
preens herself, jubilant at
the thick dazzle of bloom,
that the caught writhing has become
a sinuous wriggle of joy
beneath her fleece.

But she is working still
to feed her children,
there's a lot more yet,
bringing up all she can
a lot of goodness from roots

while the petals drop.
The fleece is gone
as suddenly as it came
and hundreds of babies are left
almost too small to be seen
but they fatten, fatten, get pink
and shine among her leaves.

Now she can repose a bit
they are so fat.
                    She cares less
birds get them, men
pick them, human children wear them
in pairs over their ears
she loses them all.
That's why she made them,
to lose them into the world, she
returns to herself,
she rests, she doesn't care.

She leans into the wind
her trunk shines black
with rain, she sleeps
as black and hard as lava.
She knows nothing about babies.

(*1976*)

D. H. Lawrence

Bare Almond-Trees

Wet almond-trees, in the rain,
Like iron sticking grimly out of earth;
Black almond trunks, in the rain,
Like iron implements twisted, hideous, out of the earth,
Out of the deep, soft fledge of Sicilian winter-green,
Earth-grass uneatable,
Almond trunks curving blackly, iron-dark, climbing the slopes.

Almond-tree, beneath the terrace rail,
Black, rusted, iron trunk,
You have welded your thin stems finer,
Like steel, like sensitive steel in the air,
Grey, lavender, sensitive steel, curving thinly and brittly up in a
  parabola.

What are you doing in the December rain?
Have you a strange electric sensitiveness in your steel tips?
Do you feel the air for electric influences
Like some strange magnetic apparatus?
Do you take in messages, in some strange code,
From heaven's wolfish, wandering electricity, that prowls so
  constantly round Etna?
Do you take the whisper of sulphur from the air?
Do you hear the chemical accents of the sun?
Do you telephone the roar of the waters over the earth?
And from all this, do you make calculations?

Sicily, December's Sicily in a mass of rain
With iron branching blackly, rusted like old, twisted implements
And brandishing and stooping over earth's wintry fledge,
  climbing the slopes
Of uneatable soft green!

TAORMINA

(*1923*)

Prunus dulcis
almond

West Asia

August Kleinzahler

Peaches in November

Peaches redden,
and at day's end glow as if lit from within
the way bronze does,

before thudding down.
Mourning doves scatter at the sound,
shooting away in low trajectories,

and the mind starts
in spite of itself, even after weeks
of hearing them drop through the night

and all day long;
the intervals so far off any possible grid
of anticipation, and the impact

each time they hit
ground amid a racket of leaves
just different enough

from the time before,
and the time before that, you are tricked
out of thought, awake

to the sound
as the last of them come down
and the boughs slowly raise themselves up.

(*1995*)

Prunus persica
peach

China

Michael Longley

The Blackthorn

A bouquet for my fifties, these flowers without leaves
Like easter snow, hailstones clustering at dayligone —
From the difficult thicket a walking stick in bloom, then
Astringency, the blackthorn and its smoky plum.

(*2000*)

Prunus spinosa
blackthorn, sloe

Europe, west Asia

Christina Rossetti

Endure Hardness

A cold wind stirs the blackthorn
  To burgeon and to blow,
Besprinkling half-green hedges
  With flakes and sprays of snow.

Thro' coldness and thro' keenness,
  Dear hearts, take comfort so:
Somewhere or other doubtless
  These make the blackthorn blow.

(*1885*, *1904*)

H. D. (Hilda Doolittle)

Pear Tree

Silver dust,
lifted from the earth,
higher than my arms reach,
you have mounted,
O silver,
higher than my arms reach
you front us with great mass;

no flower ever opened
so staunch a white leaf,
no flower ever parted silver
from such rare silver;

O white pear,
your flower-tufts
thick on the branch
bring summer and ripe fruits
in their purple hearts.

(*1916*)

Pyrus communis
pear

Europe, west Asia

Judith Wright

Words, Roses, Stars

(*for John Béchervaise, answering a Christmas poem*)

A rose, my friend, a rose —
and what's a rose?
A swirl of atoms bodied in a word.
And words are human; language comes and goes
with us, and lives among us. Not absurd
to think the human spans the Milky Way.

Baiame bends beside his crystal stream
shaded beneath his darker cypress-tree
and gives the gift of life, the endless dream,
to Koori people, and to you and me.
Astronomers and physicists compute
a mathematic glory in the sky.
But all those calculations, let's admit,
are filtered through a human brain and eye.

If I could give a rose to you, and you,
it would be language; sight and touch and scent
join in that symbol. Yet the word is true,
plucked by a path where human vision went.

(*1985*)

Rosa spp. and hybrids
rose

Northern temperate regions, Europe

W. B. Yeats

The Rose of the World

Who dreamed that beauty passes like a dream?
For these red lips, with all their mournful pride,
Mournful that no new wonder may betide,
Troy passed away in one high funeral gleam,
And Usna's children died.

We and the labouring world are passing by:
Amid men's souls, that waver and give place
Like the pale waters in their wintry race,
Under the passing stars, foam of the sky,
Lives on this lonely face.

Bow down, archangels, in your dim abode:
Before you were, or any hearts to beat,
Weary and kind one lingered by His seat;
He made the world to be a grassy road
Before her wandering feet.

(*1893*)

Hugh MacDiarmid

The Little White Rose

(*To John Gawsworth*)

The rose of all the world is not for me.
I want for my part
Only the little white rose of Scotland
That smells sharp and sweet — and breaks the heart.

(*1934*)

Rosa pimpinellifolia
burnet or Scotch rose

Eurasia

Ruth Padel

Rosa Silvestris Russica

John by Grace of God Botanist Royal,
from the British expedition
against Russia, 1618,

brings back a Russian vest.
'Stockens without heels'. Snow-boots
to walk on snow without sinking.

Soldiers die of frostbite, heartache,
diarrhoea, plague. He collates
'Things by me Observ'd',

falling most in love
with Russian roses. 'Wondros sweet'.
All the deck back

he keeps alive a Briar of Muscovy,
the ambuscad's one prize.
How else should a scientist work

but join the politicians'
raids on other worlds?
Afterwards he labours

in his South London garden
on the names of roses.
Little lights of the field.

(*1993*)

Rosa silvestris russica
briar of Muscovy

Peter Didsbury

Roses

Roses are coloured holes in the evening.
When the light fails birds fly into them.
They wriggle through to open caves
and perch on steps and ledges.
They make honest articulate parliaments.
They administer themselves until morning.

(*1982*)

W. B. Yeats

The Rose Tree

'O words are lightly spoken,'
Said Pearce to Connolly,
'Maybe a breath of politic words
Has withered our Rose Tree;
Or maybe but a wind that blows
Across the bitter sea.'

'It needs to be but watered,'
James Connolly replied,
'To make the green come out again
And spread on every side,
And shake the blossom from the bud
To be the garden's pride.'

'But where can we draw water,'
Said Pearce to Connolly,
'When all the wells are parched away?
O plain as plain can be
There's nothing but our own red blood
Can make a right Rose Tree.'

(*1916*)

Dudley Randall

Roses and Revolutions

Musing on roses and revolutions,
I saw night close down on the earth like a great dark wing,
and the lighted cities were like tapers in the night,
and I heard the lamentations of a million hearts
regretting life and crying for the grave,
and I saw the Negro lying in the swamp with his face blown off,
and in northern cities with his manhood maligned and felt the writhing
of his viscera like that of the hare hunted down or the bear at bay,
and I saw men working and taking no joy in their work
and embracing the hard-eyed whore with joyless excitement
and lying with wives and virgins in impotence.

And as I groped in darkness
and felt the pain of millions,
gradually, like day driving night across the continent,
I saw dawn upon them like the sun a vision
of a time when all men walk proudly through the earth
and the bombs and missiles lie at the bottom of the ocean
like the bones of dinosaurs buried under the shale of eras,
and men strive with each other not for power or the accumulation of paper
but in joy create for others the house, the poem, the game of athletic beauty.

Then washed in the brightness of this vision,
I saw how in its radiance would grow and be nourished and suddenly
burst into terrible and splendid bloom
the blood-red flower of revolution.

(*1966*)

Seitlhamo Motsapi

a roses for the folks we know

now i sing again
too red, the whips flake off my voice
the heart above all things
lechers too many swamps
pure pillars of unpurged babel salt
define the scarred landscape of my heart

but
the songs maul their scanty silences
fire scuttles inward over cities
cursed with forgetful walls

out of every fang a gust of love
out of every fissure seas of welcome
out of every multiplication of howls
a sprawl of sungrass singing repose

a million babygreen roses for the grace
that cushioned the unpillowed silences
between dark & dawn
a million sunblue roses for the sisterknots
of seekers singers & supplicants
whose handshaking supple cordial
hallelujahs the Lord forever
as my dungeons learn windows
seven million roses for the pikin majesties
free from philosophical corrosions
free from hate's biting smite
free from the reckless scalpels of thought

outside the city
the walls fling their profanities ever higher
immune to visions & rainbows
impervious to the ethereal epiphanies
that splinter affliction
oblivious to the thudding spirits
of incoming saints

roses for the glory
roses for the power
roses for the amens

roses for the gifts of the spirit
roses for the untangled dreams
seven million roses for the eternal oil
that surnames every togetherness
seven billion roses for the patient mountain
seven billion roses for the amiable desert
when all we could offer was one foot

for the mothers
who learned very early on
to drink from the muddy wells
between our toes
twelve million roses scented with blessings

for the sisters
who let the wind sleep in their mouths
who let madness sleep under their armpits
who let anguish grow from their gardens
twelve billion roses full of rains . . .

news riots in from the city
they tell us the walls are falling
with naked indulgences loaded onto their chariots
the heathens gallop south to shallow air
yet still
not enough gallopen roar
will sever the rose's sovereignty —
a rose for you
& for the long road
full of narrownesses
& the straggle of pilgrims

(*1995*)

Frank M. Chipasula

The Burning Rose

an elegy for Mkwapatira Mhango

You handed them a rose of truth
but they pitched it in the fire

The rose burst into *Lux in Tenebris* and raged
across the early morning lake
from Mulowe to Monkey Bay
And the rose rose and bled and fell down,
rose and bled, rose and bled, and flew
up in one raging flame that licked your house,
and ate up your wives, swallowed your children
and your guests like a rose hungry for love;
And the rose flapped against the walls
of the house that rose in flames like fiery roses;
And the rose bared its thorns in a lovely snarl,
Thorns hefty like a crazed cow's goring horns,
Hoofed with hatred, while a blazing petal
Wagged its long tongue up through the roof
And licked the children's cries
that rang like cathedral bells clanging
in the bald-headed tyrant's ears. And the rose,
Kyrie Eleison, fell like showers of clotted
blood poured in lavish libations on the kerosene
rose that bloomed from a terrible match stick.

3 January 1990

(*1991*)

Norman Nicholson

The Burning Rose

(*A Poem for Lady Day*)

Above the golden crocus climbs the rose,
  The rose that is the world's flesh and our own,
Rolled inward, folded, foliated close,
  The red bud rocking on the bright green bone.

The calyx flickers hairy fire, the tight
  Petals are frayed with flame and burn like coal;
The wicks of stamens flower into light
  And leave the shy flesh smouldering, but whole.

(*1948*)

Anonymous

'Ther Is No Rose of Swych Vertù'

Ther is no rose of swych vertù — *such excellence*
As is the rose that bare Jhesù. — *bore*

Ther is no rose of swych vertù
As is the rose that bar Jhesù; — *bore*
Alleluya.
Ther is etc.

For in this rose conteynëd was
Heven and erthe in lytyl space,
Res miranda. — *a thing to be wondered at*
Ther is etc.

Be that rose we may weel see — *by; well*
That he is God in persones thre,
Pari forma. — *in one substance*
Ther is etc.

The aungeles sung the sheperdes to: — *the angels sang to the shepherds*
'Gloria in excelcis Deo.' — *'glory to God in the highest'*
Gaudeamus. — *let us rejoice*
Ther is etc.

Leve we all this worldly merthe, — *let us leave; worldly mirth*
And folwë we this joyful berthe; — *follow; birth*
Transeamus. — *let us go*
Ther is etc.

(*c. 1450*)

Christina Rossetti

The Solitary Rose

O happy Rose, red Rose, that bloomest lonely
  Where there are none to gather while they love thee;
That are perfumed by thine own fragrance only,
  Resting like incense round thee and above thee; —
Thou hearest nought save some pure stream that flows,
      O happy Rose.

What tho' for thee no nightingales are singing?
  They chant one eve, but hush them in the morning.
Near thee no little moths and bees are winging
  To steal thy honey when the day is dawning; —
Thou keep'st thy sweetness till the twilight's close,
      O happy Rose.

Then rest in peace, thou lone and lovely flower;
  Yea be thou glad, knowing that none are near thee
To mar thy beauty in a wanton hour,
  And scatter all thy leaves, nor deign to wear thee.
Securely in thy solitude repose,
      O happy Rose.

(1847, *1896*)

Elizabeth Tollet

The Rose

Beneath my feet when Flora cast
  Her choicest sweets of various hue,
Their charms, unheeded as I passed,
  Nor cheered my sense, nor took my view.

I chose, neglecting all the rest,
  The Provence rose too fully blown.
I lodged it in my virgin breast;
  It drooped, alas, and died too soon!

This gentle sigh, this rain of eyes,
  Thy beauty never can recall:
'Tis thus that all perfection flies,
  And love and life must fade and fall.

(*1755*)

Sir Richard Fanshawe

A Rose

Blowne in the Morning, thou shalt fade ere Noone:
    What bootes a Life which in such hast forsakes thee?
    Th'art wondrous frolick being to dye so soone,
    And passing proud a little colour makes thee.

If thee thy brittle beauty so deceives,
    Know then the thing that swells thee is thy bane;
    For the same beauty doth in bloody leaves
    The sentence of thy early death containe.

Some Clownes coarse Lungs will poyson thy sweet flow'r
    If by the carelesse Plough thou shalt be torne:
    And many *Herods* lye in wait each how'r
    To murther thee as soone as thou art borne;

Nay, force thy Bud to blow; Their Tyrant breath
Anticipating Life, to hasten death.

(*1648*)

Edmund Waller

Song ('Goe Lovely Rose')

Goe lovely Rose,
Tell her that wasts her time and mee,
That now shee knowes,
When I resemble her to thee,
How sweet and fayr shee seems to bee.

Tell her that's young,
And shuns to have her graces spide,
That hadst thou sprung
In deserts where no men abide,
Thou must have uncommended dy'd.

Small is the worth
Of beauty from the light retir'd:
Bid her come forth,
Suffer her selfe to bee desir'd,
And not blush so to be admir'd.

Then dye, that shee,
The common fate of all things rare
May read in thee,
How small a part of time they share,
That are so wondrous sweet and faire.

(*1645*)

Anonymous

'Al Night by the Rosë, Rosë'

Al night by the rosë, rosë,
Al night by the rose I lay,
Dorst Ich nought the rosë stele, *dared; steal*
And yet I bar the flour away. *bore the flower*

(*c. 1325–50*)
from *The Rawlinson Lyrics*

Dora Sigerson (later Shorter)

With a Rose

In the heart of a rose
  Lies the heart of a maid;
  If you be not afraid
You will wear it. Who knows?

In the pink of its bloom,
  Lay your lips to her cheek;
  Since a rose cannot speak,
And you gain the perfume.

If the dews on the leaf
  Are the tears from her eyes;
  If she withers and dies,
Why, you have the belief,

That a rose cannot speak,
  Though the heart of a maid
  In its bosom must fade,
And with fading must break.

(*1897*)

William Blake

My Pretty Rose tree

A flower was offered to me;
Such a flower as May never bore.
But I said, I've a Pretty Rose-tree,
And I passed the sweet flower o'er.

Then I went to my Pretty Rose-tree:
To tend her by day and by night.
But my rose turnd away with jealousy:
And her thorns were my only delight.

(*1794*)

William Shakespeare

'O How Much More Doth Beautie Beautious Seeme' (Sonnet 54)

O how much more doth beautie beautious seeme,
By that sweet ornament which truth doth give,
The Rose looks faire, but fairer we it deeme
For that sweet odor which doth in it live:
The Canker bloomes have full as deepe a die,
As the perfumed tincture of the Roses,
Hang on such thornes, and play as wantonly,
When sommers breath their masked buds discloses:
But, for their virtue only is their show,
They live unwoo'd, and unrespected fade,
Die to themselves. Sweet roses doe not so,
Of their sweet deathes, are sweetest odors made:
    And so of you, beautious and lovely youth,
    When that shall fade, by verse distils your truth.

(*1609*)

Emily Dickinson

'Partake As Doth The Bee' [994]

Partake as doth the Bee,
Abstemiously.
The Rose is an Estate —
In Sicily.

(*c.* 1865, *1945*)

John Boyle O'Reilly

A White Rose

The red rose whispers of passion,
  And the white rose breathes of love;
O, the red rose is a falcon,
  And the white rose is a dove.

But I send you a cream-white rosebud,
  With a flush on its petal tips;
For the love that is purest and sweetest
  Has a kiss of desire on the lips.

(*1878*)

Dorothy Parker

One Perfect Rose

A single flow'r he sent me, since we met.
  All tenderly his messenger he chose;
Deep-hearted, pure, with scented dew still wet —
  One perfect rose.

I knew the language of the floweret;
  'My fragile leaves', it said, 'his heart enclose'.
Love long has taken for his amulet
  One perfect rose.

Why is it no one ever sent me yet
  One perfect limousine, do you suppose?
Ah no, it's always just my luck to get
  One perfect rose.

(*1926*)

Fred Voss

A Threat

My fellow workers and I
operate machines that cut steel blocks.

As the machines cut the steel,
my fellow workers like to stare and laugh at each other.
They are ready to piss on each other's graves.

They fear me.
They call me crazy.
They don't like the poetry I read.
They don't like the paintings I have hung
on the board behind my machine.
They look at me
like they want to cut my balls off.

Tomorrow I think I will start bringing roses to work.
Each day I will stand a rose in a jar of water
on the workbench behind my machine.
I want to really terrify my fellow workers
this time.

(*1998*)

Fred D'Aguiar

A Gift of a Rose

Two policemen (I remember there were at least two)
stopped me and gave me a bunch of red, red roses.
I nursed them with ice and water mixed with soluble aspirin.
The roses had an instant bloom attracting stares
and children who pointed; toddlers cried and ran.

This is not the season for roses, everyone said,
you must have done something to procure them.
I argued I was simply flashed down and the roses
liberally spread over my face and body to epithets
sworn by the police in praise of my black skin and mother.

Others told me to take care of the flowers, photo them,
a rare species, an example for others, a statistic;
that the policemen should be made a return gift
crossed several minds — a rose for a rose.
With neglect, they shrivelled and disappeared,

people stopped looking when I went saturday shopping.
Though I was deflowered, a rose memory burned clear.
Now when I see the police ahead, I take the first exit;
I even fancy I have a bouquet of my own for them;
I pray they'll keep their unseasonable gifts to themselves.

(*1993*)

Anne Sexton

Red Roses

Tommy is three and when he's bad
his mother dances with him.
She puts on the record,
'Red Roses for a Blue Lady'
and throws him across the room.
Mind you,
she never laid a hand on him,
only the wall laid a hand on him.
He gets red roses in different places,
the head, that time he was sleepy as a river,
the back, that time he was a broken scarecrow,
the arm like a diamond had bitten it,
the leg, twisted like a licorice stick,
all the dance they did together,
Blue Lady and Tommy.
You fell, she said, just remember you fell.
I fell, is all he told the doctors
in the big hospital. A nice lady came
and asked him questions but because
he didn't want to be sent away he said, I fell.
He never said anything else although he could talk fine.
He never told about the music
or how she'd sing and shout
holding him up and throwing him.

He pretends he is her ball.
He tries to fold up and bounce
but he squashes like fruit.
For he loves Blue Lady and the spots
of red red roses he gives her.

(*1976*)

Alice Fulton

Rose Fever

Believing even an infant's primrose
pout devours what's sweet
and smaller than itself,
how can I surrender
to your embouchure
rippling all my pores?
Beneath raw silk, my thighs
tighten to a secretive frieze.

In restaurants you gargle
the champagne, all antics
and no manners, going home
dawdle on corners looking for cripples
to boost across: good,
too good. I know you
swiped these 12 long-stems
from some blind vendor. You're a knave
of hearts & now you've got me

crooning across dining rooms
and avenues, sniffing out
your soul where it dapples through
the shy skin circling your navel.
The solstice lengthens to a sexual pink,
pavement swoons between its curbs:

all my dark parts
itch with rose fever.
In a limp rally, I learn
the world's catcalls
by rote, thinking to note them
in your spell. See, I'm sound
in body but weak in belief,
caught in this airtight intersection
wanting to give in, gasping.

Lend me your gift
for plunder so I can blaze a way
through the shrapnel and the rapture.
Open your eyes and let me see

the innocent within,
his palms extended like a sharing.
Just slip me one unstudied look
before the retina sounds
its blue alert.

(*1983*)

William Blake

The Sick Rose

O Rose thou art sick.
The invisible worm
That flies in the night
In the howling storm:

Has found out thy bed
Of crimson joy:
And his dark secret love
Does thy life destroy.

(*1794*)

Muriel Rukeyser

Fighting for Roses

After the last freeze, in easy air,
Once the danger is past, we cut them back severely;
Pruning the weakest hardest, pruning for size
Of flower, we deprived will not deprive the sturdy.
The new shoots are preserved, the future bush
Cut down to a couple of young dormant buds.

But the early sun of April does not burn our lives:
Light straight and fiery brings back the enemies.
Claw, jaw, and crawler, all those that devour.
We work with smoke against the robber blights,
With copper against rust; the season fights itself
In deep strong rich loam under swarm attacks.

Head hidden from the wind, the power of form
Rises among these brightnesses, thorned and blowing.
Where they glow on the earth, water-drops tremble on them.
Soon we must cut them back, against damage of storms.
But those days gave us flower budded on flower,
A moment of light achieved, deep in the air of roses.

(*1968*)

Raymond Carver

Cherish

From the window I see her bend to the roses
holding close to the bloom so as not to
prick her fingers. With the other hand she clips, pauses and
clips, more alone in the world
than I had known. She won't
look up, not now. She's alone
with roses and with something else I can only think, not
say. I know the names of those bushes

given for our late wedding: Love, Honor, Cherish —
this last the rose she holds out to me suddenly, having
entered the house between glances. I press
my nose to it, draw the sweetness in, let it cling — scent
of promise, of treasure. My hand on her wrist to bring her close,
her eyes green as river-moss. Saying it then, against
what comes: *wife*, while I can, while my breath, each hurried
petal
can still find her.

(*1989*)

Ian Hamilton

Rose

In the delicately shrouded heart
Of this white rose, a patient eye,
The eye of love,
Knows who I am, and where I've been
Tonight, and what I wish I'd done.

I have been watching this white rose
For hours, imagining
Each tremor of each petal to be like a breath
That silences and soothes.
'Look at it', I'd say to you
If you were here: 'it is a sign
Of what is brief, and lonely
And in love.'

But you have gone and so I'll call it wise:
A patient breath, an eye, a rose
That opens up too easily, and dies.

(*1987*)

Rubiaceae: Coffee family

August Kleinzahler

The Gardenia

Corinna in May pushed a rusty nail
deep in the soil of her sick gardenia.

All through the rain months leaf tips curled.
What buds appeared were sickly pale.
As a consumptive heroine in winter light
so fared and failed Corinna's plant.

In June beside the burbling toilet,
a dark shellac arose in the leaves.
A bud grew fat and began to peel.
The pedicel swelled.

At last came the bloom.

Corinna of the milky thighs
unfastened her wrapper and drew a bath
so that she might wash, dream
then wash herself again

that warm spring night in the fragrant room.

(*1989*)

Gardenia augusta
gardenia

China

James Schuyler

The Bluet

And is it stamina
that unseasonably freaks
forth a bluet, a
Quaker lady, by
the lake? So small,
a drop of sky that
splashed and held,
four-petalled, creamy
in its throat. The woods
around were brown,
the air crisp as a
Carr's table water
biscuit and smelt of
cider. There were frost
apples on the trees in
the field below the house.
The pond was still then
broke into a ripple.
The hills, the leaves that
have not yet fallen
are deep and oriental
rug colors. Brown leaves
in the woods set off
gray trunks of trees.
But that bluet was
the focus of it all: last
spring, next spring, what
does it matter? Unexpected
as a tear when someone
reads a poem you wrote
for him: 'It's this line

here'. That bluet breaks
me up, tiny spring flower
late, late in dour October.

(*1974*)

Hedyotis caerulea
bluet

North America

Salicaceae: Willow family

Seamus Heaney

The Poplar

Wind shakes the big poplar, quicksilvering
The whole tree in a single sweep.
What bright scale fell and left this needle quivering?
What loaded balances have come to grief?

(*1996*)

Populus alba
white poplar

Eurasia, North Africa

Mimi Khalvati

'Why Does the Aspen Tremble?'

Why does the aspen tremble
  without a trace of wind?
Under its spire, close
  your eyes, listen.
Listen to Khadijah. Her
  big heart beating.
He is bringing a new wife
  home today. Half her age.
Twice her beauty. Aisha, Aisha.
  Listen to the leaves.
What the Bosnian Moslem women say.
  The story they weave.

Khadijah is not jealous.
  Under the awning she
stands, arms folded
  Arms she will open wide.
Large, generous Khadijah
  ample-limbed . . .
But when a horse
  pricks up its ears, backs
two paces, whinnies, a current
  faint as the morning star
runs through her, air around her
  ripples, stills.

Like an arrow loosed from
  a quiver, that impulse
shot from her heart
  is caught in the arms
of aspen, sends a shiver
  through every leaf.
And thereafter, though there are
  no aspens in Arabia
though there is

no wind, this is why
the aspen trembles
over the bed's thin stream.

(Khadijah was the Prophet Mohammed's first wife and Aisha his third, though he did not marry her until after Khadijah's death. MK)

(1997)

Populus tremula
aspen

Eurasia, North Africa

Edward Thomas

Aspens

All day and night, save winter, every weather,
Above the inn, the smithy, and the shop,
The aspens at the cross-roads talk together
Of rain, until their last leaves fall from the top.

Out of the blacksmith's cavern comes the ringing
Of hammer, shoe, and anvil; out of the inn
The clink, the hum, the roar, the random singing —
The sounds that for these fifty years have been.

The whisper of the aspens is not drowned,
And over lightless pane and footless road,
Empty as sky, with every other sound
Not ceasing, calls their ghosts from their abode,

A silent smithy, a silent inn, nor fails
In the bare moonlight or the thick-furred gloom,
In tempest or the night of nightingales,
To turn the cross-roads to a ghostly room.

And it would be the same were no house near.
Over all sorts of weather, men, and times,
Aspens must shake their leaves and men may hear
But need not listen, more than to my rhymes.

Whatever wind blows, while they and I have leaves
We cannot other than an aspen be
That ceaselessly, unreasonably grieves,
Or so men think who like a different tree.

(*1916*)

Gerard Manley Hopkins

Binsey Poplars

felled 1879

My aspens dear, whose airy cages quelled,
Quelled or quenched in leaves the leaping sun,
All felled, felled, are all felled;
        Of a fresh and following folded rank
                Not spared, not one
                That dandled a sandalled
            Shadow that swam or sank
On meadow and river and wind-wandering weed-winding bank.

O if we but knew what we do
            When we delve or hew —
        Hack and rack the growing green!
            Since country is so tender
        To touch, her being só slender,
        That, like this sleek and seeing ball
        But a prick will make no eye at all,
          Where we, even when we mean
              To mend her we end her,
              When we hew or delve:
After-comers cannot guess the beauty been.
        Ten or twelve, only ten or twelve
          Strokes of havoc únselve
              The sweet especial scene,
        Rural scene, a rural scene,
        Sweet especial rural scene.

(1879, *1918*)

William Cowper

The Poplar-Field

The poplars are felled; farewell to the shade
And the whispering sound of the cool colonnade;
The winds play no longer and sing in the leaves.
Nor Ouse on his bosom their image receives.

Twelve years have elapsed since I first took a view
Of my favourite field, and the bank where they grew;
And now in the grass behold they are laid,
And the tree is my seat that once lent me a shade.

The blackbird has fled to another retreat
Where the hazels afford him a screen from the heat.
And the scene where his melody charmed me before
Resounds with his sweet-flowing ditty no more.

My fugitive years are all hasting away,
And I must ere long lie as lowly as they
With a turf on my breast, and a stone at my head,
Ere another such grove shall arise in its stead.

'Tis a sight to engage me, if anything can,
To muse on the perishing pleasures of man;
Though his life be a dream, his enjoyments, I see,
Have a being less durable even than he.

(*1785*)

Populus spp.
poplar

Northern temperate regions, Europe

Robert Herrick

To the Willow-tree

1. Thou art to all love lost the best,
The onely true plant found,
Wherewith young men and maids distrest,
And left of love, are crown'd.

2. When once the Lover's Rose is dead,
Or laid aside forlorne;
Then Willow-garlands 'bout the head,
Bedew'd with teares are worne.

3. When with Neglect, (the Lovers' bane)
Poore Maids rewarded be
For their love lost; their onely gaine
Is but a Wreathe from thee.

4. And underneath thy cooling shade,
(When weary of the light)
The love-spent Youth, and love-sick Maid,
Come to weep out the night.

(*1648*)

Salix babylonica
willow

Probable origin: China

Sapotaceae: Sapodilla family

Olive Senior

Starapple

Expect no windfall here.
Don't stand and wait
    at this portal between
shadow and light.
Two-sided starapple leaf
    can't be trusted as guide.
Without force, starapple
    won't let go of its fruit.
Too afraid you'll discover
    the star already fallen
    the apple compromised.

(*1995*)

Chrysophyllum cainito
starapple

Tropical America

Scrophulariaceae: Figwort family

Ted Hughes

Sunstruck Foxglove

As you bend to touch
The gypsy girl
Who waits for you in the hedge
Her loose dress falls open.

Midsummer ditch-sickness!

Flushed, freckled with earth-fever,
Swollen lips parted, her eyes closing,
A lolling armful, and so young! Hot

Among the insane spiders.
You glimpse the reptile under-speckle
Of her sunburned breasts
And your head swims. You close your eyes.

Can the foxes talk? Your head throbs.
Remember the bird's tolling echo,
The dripping fern-roots, and the butterfly touches
That woke you.

Remember your mother's
Long, dark dugs.

Her silky body a soft oven
For loaves of pollen.

(*1986*)

Digitalis purpurea
foxglove

Mediterranean; the homogenous northern European population expanded from the Iberian peninsula after the last Ice Age

Lizette Woodworth Reese

A Flower of Mullein

I am too near, too clear a thing for you,
A flower of mullein in a crack of wall,
The villagers half-see, or not at all,
Part of the weather, like the wind or dew.
You love to pluck the different, and find
Stuff for your joy in cloudy loveliness;
You love to fumble at a door, and guess
At some strange happening that may wait behind.
Yet life is full of tricks, and it is plain
That men drift back to some worn field or roof,
To grip at comfort in a room, a stair;
To warm themselves at some flower down a lane:
You, too, may long, grown tired of the aloof,
For the sweet surety of the common air.

(*1926*)

Verbascum thapsus
mullein, Aaron's rod, flannel plant, hag-taper

Eurasia, naturalised in North America

Solanaceae: Potato family

Thom Gunn

Mandrakes

look for us among those
shy flowers opening
at night only
                    in the
shadow, in the held breath
under oaktrees listen for

rootshuffle or is it wind
  you won't find us, we
got small a long time back
we withdrew like the Picts
into fireside tale and rumour

we were terrible in our time
gaunt plants fertilized
by the leachings of hanged men
  knobby frames shrieking and
stumping around the planet

smaller and bushier now
prudent green men moving
in oakshadow or among reed
guardians of the young snake
          rearing from the water
          with the head and curving
          neck of a small dinosaur

we can outwait you for
ever if we need, lounging
leafy arms linked along
some park's path, damp fallen leaves
covering our itch to move

mouths open to the wind
sough entering sigh

into fireside tale and rumour

(*1983*)

Mandragora officinarum
mandrake

South Europe

Jay Macpherson

Mandrake

The fall from man engenders me,
Rooted beneath the deadly tree.
My certain origin I show,
Single above and forked below.
Man grubs me from my peaceful sink
To aid his horrid loves, and link
My fate more strongly with his own:
Foreknowledge racks me, and I groan.

(*1981*)

Steruliaceae: Cocoa family

Judith Wright

Flame-Tree in a Quarry

From the broken bone of the hill
stripped and left for dead,
like a wrecked skull,
leaps out this bush of blood.

Out of the torn earth's mouth
comes the old cry of praise.
Still is the song made flesh
though the singer dies —

flesh of the world's delight,
voice of the world's desire,
I drink you with my sight
and I am filled with fire.

Out of the very wound
springs up this scarlet breath —
this fountain of hot joy,
this living ghost of death.

(*1949*)

Brachychiton acerifolius
flame-tree

North-east Australia

Taxaceae: Yew family

Alfred, Lord Tennyson

'Old Yew, Which Graspest at the Stones'

Old yew, which graspest at the stones
  That name the under-lying dead,
  Thy fibres net the dreamless head,
Thy roots are wrapt about the bones.

The seasons bring the flower again,
  And bring the firstling to the flock;
  And in the dusk of thee, the clock
Beats out the little lives of men.

O, not for thee the glow, the bloom,
  Who changest not in any gale,
  Nor branding summer suns avail
To touch thy thousand years of gloom;

And gazing on thee, sullen tree,
  Sick for thy stubborn hardihood,
  I seem to fall from out my blood
And grow incorporate into thee.

(*1850*)

from *In Memoriam A.H.H.*

Taxus baccata
yew

Europe and the Mediterranean

Tiliaceae: Lime-Tree family

Samuel Taylor Coleridge

This Lime-Tree Bower My Prison

Well, they are gone, and here must I remain,
This lime-tree bower my prison! I have lost
Beauties and feelings, such as would have been
Most sweet to my remembrance even when age
Had dimmed mine eyes to blindness! They, meanwhile,
Friends, whom I never more may meet again,
On springy heath, along the hill-top edge,
Wander in gladness, and wind down, perchance,
To that still roaring dell, of which I told;
The roaring dell, o'erwooded, narrow, deep,
And only speckled by the mid-day sun;
Where its slim trunk the ash from rock to rock
Flings arching like a bridge — that branchless ash,
Unsunn'd and damp, whose few poor yellow leaves
Ne'er tremble in the gale, yet tremble still,
Fanned by the water-fall! and there my friends
Behold the dark green file of long lank weeds,
That all at once (a most fantastic sight!)
Still nod and drip beneath the dripping edge
Of the blue clay-stone.

Now, my friends emerge
Beneath the wide wide Heaven — and view again
The many-steepled tract magnificent
Of hilly fields and meadows, and the sea,
With some fair bark, perhaps, whose sails light up
The slip of smooth clear blue betwixt two Isles
Of purple shadow! Yes! they wander on
In gladness all; but thou, methinks, most glad,
My gentle-hearted Charles! for thou hast pined
And hungered after Nature, many a year,
In the great City pent, winning thy way
With sad yet patient soul, through evil and pain

And strange calamity! Ah! slowly sink
Behind the western ridge, thou glorious Sun!
Shine in the slant beams of the sinking orb,
Ye purple heath-flowers! richlier burn, ye clouds!
Live in the yellow light, ye distant groves!
And kindle, thou blue Ocean! So my friend
Struck with deep joy may stand, as I have stood,
Silent with swimming sense; yea, gazing round
On the wide landscape, gaze till all doth seem
Less gross than bodily; and of such hues
As veil the Almighty Spirit, when yet he makes
Spirits perceive his presence.

A delight
Comes sudden on my heart, and I am glad
As I myself were there! Nor in this bower,
This little lime-tree bower, have I not mark'd
Much that has sooth'd me. Pale beneath the blaze
Hung the transparent foliage; and I watch'd
Some broad and sunny leaf, and lov'd to see
The shadow of the leaf and stem above
Dappling its sunshine! And that walnut-tree
Was richly ting'd, and a deep radiance lay
Full on the ancient ivy, which usurps
Those fronting elms, and now, with blackest mass
Makes their dark branches gleam a lighter hue
Through the late twilight: and though now the bat
Wheels silent by, and not a swallow twitters,
Yet still the solitary humble-bee
Sings in the bean-flower! Henceforth I shall know
That Nature ne'er deserts the wise and pure;
No plot so narrow, be but Nature there,
No waste so vacant, but may well employ
Each faculty of sense, and keep the heart
Awake to Love and Beauty! and sometimes
'Tis well to be bereft of promis'd good,
That we may lift the soul, and contemplate
With lively joy the joys we cannot share.
My gentle-hearted Charles! when the last rook
Beat its straight path along the dusky air
Homewards, I blest it! deeming, its black wing
(Now a dim speck, now vanishing in light)

Had cross'd the mighty Orb's dilated glory,
While thou stood'st gazing; or when all was still,
Flew creeking o'er thy head, and had a charm
For thee, my gentle-hearted Charles, to whom
No sound is dissonant which tells of Life.

(*1834*)

Tilia cordata
small-leaved lime-tree

Europe
Formerly the most important tree in lowland England, characterising the original forest; the last major tree to enter the country after the Ice Age, not reaching Ireland or Scotland — the seeds were sterile in north-west England, as it was too cold for successful fertilisation

Amy Clampitt

Lindenbloom

Before midsummer density
opaques with shade the checker-
tables underneath, in daylight
unleafing lindens burn
green-gold a day or two,
no more, with intimations
of an essence I saw once,
in what had been the pleasure-
garden of the popes
at Avignon, dishevel

into half (or possibly three-
quarters of) a million
hanging, intricately
tactile, blond bell-pulls
of bloom, the in-mid-air
resort of honeybees'
hirsute cotillion
teasing by the milligram
out of those necklaced
nectaries, aromas

so intensely subtle,
strollers passing under
looked up confused,
as though they'd just
heard voices, or
inhaled the ghost
of derelict splendor
and/or of seraphs shaken
into pollen dust

no transubstantiating
pope or antipope could sift
or quite precisely ponder.

(*1983*)

Tilia × *europaea*
linden, lime

Europe to south-west Asia
Natural hybrid

Trilliaceae: Wake-Robin family

Louise Glück

Trillium

When I woke up I was in a forest. The dark
seemed natural, the sky through the pine trees
thick with many lights.

I knew nothing; I could do nothing but see.
And as I watched, all the lights of heaven
faded to make a single thing, a fire
burning through the cool firs.
Then it wasn't possible any longer
to stare at heaven and not be destroyed.

Are there souls that need
death's presence, as I require protection?
I think if I speak long enough
I will answer that question, I will see
whatever they see, a ladder
reaching through the firs, whatever
calls them to exchange their lives —

Think what I understand already.
I woke up ignorant in a forest;
only a moment ago, I didn't know my voice
if one were given me
would be so full of grief, my sentences
like cries strung together.

I didn't even know I felt grief
until that word came, until I felt
rain streaming from me.

(*1992*)

Trillium spp.
Trinity flower, wake-robin, birthroot, stinking Benjamin

North America (especially South Appalachians), Himalayas, east Asia

Ulmaceae: Elm-Tree family

C. K. Williams

Elms

All morning the tree men have been taking down the stricken
elms skirting the broad sidewalks.
The pitiless electric chain saws whine tirelessly up and down
their piercing, operatic scales
and the diesel choppers in the street shredding the debris chug
feverishly, incessantly,
packing truckload after truckload with the feathery,
homogenized, inert remains of heartwood,
twig and leaf and soon the block is stripped, it is as though
illusions of reality were stripped:
the rows of naked facing buildings stare and think, their
divagations more urgent than they were.
'The winds of time,' they think, the mystery charged with fearful
clarity: 'The winds of time . . .'
All afternoon, on to the unhealing evening, minds racing,
'Insolent, unconscionable, the winds of time . . .'

(*1995*)

Ulmus spp.
elm

Northern temperate regions to North Mexico, Europe

Umbelliferae: Carrot family

William Carlos Williams

Queen-Ann's-Lace

Her body is not so white as
anemone petals nor so smooth — nor
so remote a thing. It is a field
of the wild carrot taking
the field by force; the grass
does not raise above it.
Here is no question of whiteness,
white as can be, with a purple mole
at the center of each flower.
Each flower is a hand's span
of her whiteness. Wherever
his hand has lain there is
a tiny purple blemish. Each part
is a blossom under his touch
to which the fibres of her being
stem one by one, each to its end,
until the whole field is a
white desire, empty, a single stem,
a cluster, flower by flower,
a pious wish to whiteness gone over —
or nothing.

(*1925*)

Anthriscus sylvestris
cow-parsley

Eurasia, Europe, African mountains

Urticaceae: Nettle family

Edward Thomas

Tall Nettles

Tall nettles cover up, as they have done
These many springs, the rusty harrow, the plough
Long worn out, and the roller made of stone:
Only the elm butt tops the nettles now.

This corner of the farmyard I like most:
As well as any bloom upon a flower
I like the dust on the nettles, never lost
Except to prove the sweetness of a shower.

(*1917*)

Urtica dioica
nettle

Eurasia

A. E. Housman

'It Nods and Curtseys and Recovers'

It nods and curtseys and recovers
  When the wind blows above,
The nettle on the grave of lovers
  That hanged themselves for love.

The nettle nods, the wind blows over,
  The man, he does not move,
The lover of the grave, the lover
  That hanged himself for love.

(*1896*)

Violaceae: Violet family

Ruth Pitter

The Tuft of Violets

Our solitary larch
Spread her green silk against the south,
When late-relenting March
Ended the sowing-time of welcome drouth;
And from the bank beneath
Sheltered by budding hedge and bowing tree,
A moist delicious breath
Of rainy violets came out to me.

There was the healthy mass
Of dark delightful leaves, with their own breath
Of silvan moss and grass;
But all among and over them there went

The sweetness lovers know,
And age will pause upon, while time returns,
And earlier violets grow
In a lost kingdom where no creature mourns.

From high above my head
The mated missel-thrush was singing proudly,
And through that dusky bed
The light-reflecting bee rejoicing loudly,
Kissing each modest face,
Sang to them well how beautiful they were,
Who in that slight embrace
Let fall upon the green a little tear.

Time ceased, as if the spring
Had been eternity; I had no age;
The purple and the wing
That visited and hymned it, were a page
Royally dyed, written in gold;

Royal with truth, for ever springing;
For ever, as of old,
The sunlight and the darkness and the singing.

(*1953*)

Viola spp.
violet

Temperate regions, especially northern hemisphere, Europe and Andes

Robert Herrick

To Violets

1. Welcome Maids of Honour,
        You doe bring
        In the Spring;
   And wait upon her.

2. She has Virgins many,
        Fresh and faire;
        Yet you are
   More sweet than any.

3. Y'are the Maiden Posies,
        And so grac't
        To be plac't
   'Fore Damask Roses.

4. Yet though thus respected,
        By and by
        Ye doe lie,
   Poore Girles, neglected.

(*1648*)

Christina Rossetti

Autumn Violets

Keep love for youth, and violets for the spring:
  Or if these bloom when worn-out autumn grieves,
  Let them lie hid in double shade of leaves,
Their own, and others dropped down withering;
For violets suit when home birds build and sing,
  Not when the outbound bird a passage cleaves;
  Not with dry stubble of mown harvest sheaves,
But when the green world buds to blossoming.
Keep violets for the spring, and love for youth,
  Love that should dwell with beauty, mirth and hope:
    Or if a later sadder love be born,
  Let this not look for grace beyond its scope,
But give itself, nor plead for answering truth —
    A graceful Ruth tho' gleaning scanty corn.

(*1868 1904*)

Stanley Kunitz

Approach of Autumn

The early violets we saw together,
Lifting their delicate swift heads
As if to dip them in the water, now wither,
Arching no more like thoroughbreds.

Slender and pale, they flee the rime
Of death: the ghosts of violets
Are running in a dream. Heart-flowering time
Decays, green goes, and the eye forgets.

Forgets? But what spring-blooded stock
Sprouts deathless violets in the skull,
That, pawing on the hard and bitter rock
Of reason, make thinking beautiful?

(*1930*)

Derek Walcott

The Harvest

If they ask what my favourite flower was,
there's one thing that you'll have to understand:
I learnt to love it by the usual ways
of those who swore to serve truth with one hand,
and one behind their back for cash or praise,
that I surrendered dreaming how I'd stand
in the rewarding autumn of my life,
just ankle-deep in money, thick as leaves,
to bring my poetry, poor, faithful wife
past her accustomed style, well, all the same,
though there's no autumn, nature played the game
with me each fiscal year, when the gold pouis
would guiltily start scattering largesse
like Christian bankers or wind-shook-down thieves.
What I soon learnt was they had changed the script,
left out the golden fall and turned to winter,
to some grey monochrome, much like this metre,
with no gold in it. So, I saw my toil
as a seedy little yard of scrub and root
that gripped for good, and what took in that soil,
was the cheap flower that you see at my foot,
the coarsest, commonest, toughest, nondescript,
resilient violet with its white spot centre.

(*1976*)

John Clare

March Violet

Where last year's leaves and weeds decay
  March violets are in blow,
I'd rake the rubbish all away
  And give them room to grow.

Near neighbours to the arum proud,
  Where dewdrops fall and sleep,
As purple as a fallen cloud,
  March violets bloom and creep.

Scenting the gales of early morn,
  They smell before they're seen,
Peeping beneath the old whitethorn
  That shows its tender green.

The lamb will nibble by their bloom
  And eat them day by day,
Till briars forbid his steps to come,
  And then he skips away.

Mid nettle stalks that wither there
  And on the greensward die,
All bleaching in the thin March air
  The scattered violets lie.

(1842–64, *1935*)

Viola odorata
sweet violet

Eurasia to Africa

Michael Longley

Heartsease

When Helen, destroyer of cities, destroyer of men,
Slipped the lads a Mickey Finn of wine and heartsease,
Unhappiness's cure, a painkiller strong enough
To keep you dry-eyed for a day even if mummy
Or daddy pegs out, or your brother or son's bumped off
On the doorstep in front of you (an Egyptian drug?),
She hadn't a clue that where I hail from — beyond
The north wind, Hyperborean, or nearly — heartsease
Is kiss-me-quick, kiss-me-behind-the-garden-gate,
That in Donegal this pansy gets mixed up with selfheal.

(*2000*)

Viola tricolor
heartsease, love-in-idleness, Johnny-jump-up

Europe, naturalised in North America

Walter Savage Landor

Hearts-Ease

There is a flower I wish to wear,
  But not until first worne by you . . .
Hearts-ease . . . of all Earth's flowers most rare;
  Bring it; and bring enough for two.

(*1846*)

Sharon Olds

My Mother's Pansies

And all that time, in back of the house,
there were pansies growing, some silt blue,
some silt yellow, most of them sable
red or purplish sable, heavy
as velvet curtains, so soft they seemed wet but they were
dry as powder on a luna's wing,
dust on an alluvial path, in a drought
summer. And they were open like lips,
and pouted like lips, and had a tiny fur-gold
v, which made bees not be able
to not want. And so, although women, in our
lobes and sepals, our corollas and spurs, seemed
despised spathe, style-arm, standard,
crest, and fall,
still there were those plush entries,
night mouth, pillow mouth,
anyone might want to push
their pinky, or anything, into such velveteen
chambers, such throats, each midnight-velvet
petal saying touch-touch-touch, please-touch, please-touch,
each sex like a spirit — shy, flushed, praying.

(*2000*)

Viola × *wittrockiana*
pansy

Garden hybrid, raised 1830

Vitaceae: Vine family

Robin Robertson

Making the Green One Red

The Virginia creeper has built its church here
in the apple tree: vermilion
lacework, pennons, tendrils
of scarlet and amber
hung through the host like veins.
Spangled and jaspered, shot with red,
the tree filled with sun is stained glass:
a cathedral of blood and gold.

It took me years to find the creeper's roots,
knotted in a mulch of leaves and the fallen,
forgotten fruit: the arms espaliered
like Christ to the garden wall. Its red
has reached this first-floor window now,
the apple tree is dead.

(*2001*)

Parthenocissus quinquefolia
Virginia creeper

North-east United States to Mexico

Zygophyllaceae: Creosote-Bush family

Edward Baugh

Lignum Vitae

When the final carry-down artist lock down
this town and scorch the earth till not
even lizard don't crawl, those who still living
next morning will see me surviving still
wood of life, salvation tree
I renew my phases of lilac-blue
and gold and always green, I am
a shady place for those who have lost
their way to the house of the man who gave
them stones for bread.
                                        I don't want to sound
like I boasting, but too many small men in this two-
by-four place is giant, and you only have to open
your mouth and you can hang up a shingle outside
your gate with 'expert' behind your name.
And to think, so many people born
and grow and dead and never feel
the rainbreeze blowing cool across
Chinchona from Catherine's Peak at middle
day. Sometimes I feel my heart
harden, but I not going nowhere, my root
sink too deep, and when the 8 o'clock sun

wake up the generations of stale pee and puke
that stain the sidewalk by Parade, I weep
I bloom choirs of small butterflies.

(*1988*)

Guaiacum officinale
creosote bush

Tropical Americas, Jamaica
The hardest of commercially used timbers; almost exterminated because of intensive medicinal use in venereal disease; introduced to Spain in 1501 and used with mercury in Europe in the treatment of syphilis

Acknowledgements

Special love to my Mum who taught me the names of flowers and trees and read me poetry when I was very small, put up with my muddy boots during my years as a gardener, and who has always supported my uncertain lifestyle as a poet.

Heartfelt thanks to Andrew Dilger, August Kleinzahler, Caroline Williams, Crispin Hughes, Dipo Agboluaje, Katherine Pierpoint, Kathleen Jamie, Jane Duran, Jo Oyediran, Joe Williams, Lemn Sissay, Meg Errington, Mimi Khalvati, Nick Downing, Ruth Goodwin, Sally Read, Seitlhamo Motsapi, Sharon Morris, Veronica Ryan and Zakaria Mohammed, without whose love and support through both hard times and good, *Flora Poetica* never would have made it into the world.

Many thanks to everyone at Chelsea Physic Garden, especially Dawn Sanders, the Education Officer, for getting me to Marrakesh and back; Sue Minter, the Curator, for encouraging my residency; and Fiona Crumley, Head Gardener, for permitting strange objects to be planted in her Order Beds. Thanks also to Christina Patterson at the Poetry Society for her essential support.

Rebecca Carter, my delightful and supportive editor at Chatto, transformed the Introduction of this book from a convoluted thesis into a readable piece of prose. Thanks also to Penelope Hoare for commissioning the anthology, and to Alison Samuel for her enthusiasm and commitment.

Most of the research for the book was carried out in the British Library. I'd like to thank all the staff – the library assistants, cloakroom attendants and security guards – whose warmth and good humour make working in the BL a real pleasure, despite their pitiful wages. Special thanks to Kwame Ababio in Rare Books and Carlos Corbin in Maps.

Nick Downing came up with the title *Flora Poetica* and helped me with the proofs: well beyond the call of friendship and very much appreciated. Nick Wetton provided me with invaluable guidance and support with clearing permissions for the poems; and Simon Kovesi helped me negotiate the minefield of the copyright to John Clare's poems.

One of the greatest pleasures of editing *Flora Poetica* was the enthusiastic and generous responses of all the poets I contacted for permission to use their work. Moniza Alvi, Rita Dove, Alice Fulton, Louise Glück, Jorie Graham, Selima Hill, Kathleen Jamie, Mimi Khalvati, August Kleinzahler, James Lasdun, Philip Levine, Michael Longley, Christopher Middleton, Blake Morrison, Les Murray, James Reiss, Adrienne Rich, Anne Ridler, Myrna Stone and Richard Wilbur were kind enough to waive their fees. Sadly, the generosity of other poets will come too late to be recorded here: but thank you, one and all. The kindness of many other copyright holders is also much appreciated. Thanks also to Lorna Goodison, Sandra McPherson and Seni Seneviratne. Les Murray, Kathleen Jamie and Robin Robertson gave me unpublished poems. Much to our mutual astonishment, Don Paterson actually wrote 'Twinflooer' at my request; thanks, pal.

Seitlhamo Motsapi knows what this means: *love.*

For permission to reprint copyright material, the editor and Chatto & Windus gratefully acknowledge the following:

LIONEL ABRAHAMS: 'After Winter '76' from *Journal of a New Man* (A. D. Donker, 1984); **JOHN AGARD**: 'Palm Tree King' from *Palm Tree King* (Pluto Press, 1993), reprinted by permission of John Agard c/o Caroline Sheldon Literary Agency; **MEENA ALEXANDER**: 'Jasmine' from *Stone Roots* (Arnold-Heinemann, 1980); **MONIZA ALVI**: 'Hydrangeas' from *Carrying My Wife* (Bloodaxe Books, 2000), reprinted by permission of the author and publisher; **A. R. AMMONS**: 'Holly' from *The Selected Poems: Expanded Edition* (Norton, 1986), © 1987, 1977, 1975, 1974, 1972, 1971, 1970, 1966, 1965, 1964, 1955 by A. R. Ammons, reprinted by permission of W. W. Norton & Company Inc; **MARGARET ATWOOD**: 'Squaw Lilies: Some Notes' from *Poems 1976–1986* (Virago, 1992), reprinted by permission of Little, Brown & Company (UK); **EDWARD BAUGH**: 'Lignum Vitae' from *It Was The Singing* (Sandberry Press, 2000), reprinted by permission of the publisher; **JAMES BAXTER**: 'The Ngaio Tree' from *Collected Poems* (Oxford University Press, New Zealand, 1979), reprinted by permission of J. C. Baxter; **JOHN BURNSIDE**: 'Russian Vine' from *Angels and Animals* (Sheepwash Press, 2000), reprinted by permission of the author; **ROY CAMPBELL**:

'Autumn Plane' and 'The Palm' from *Selected Poems* (Oxford University Press, 1982), reprinted by permission of Jonathan Ball Publishers; **RAYMOND CARVER**: 'Cherish' from *A New Path to the Waterfall* (Collins Harvill, 1989) © the Estate of Raymond Carver, reprinted by permission of the Estate of Raymond Carver c/o Rogers Coleride & White, 20 Powis Mews, London W11 1JN in association with International Creative Management, New York; **FRANK CHIPASULA**: 'The Burning Rose' from *Whispers in the Wings* (Heinemann, 1991); **AMY CLAMPITT**: 'Botanical Nomenclature' and 'Lindenbloom' from *The Kingfisher* (Faber & Faber, 1983), and 'Fireweed' and 'Vacant Lot with Pokeweed' from *Westward* (Faber & Faber, 1991), reprinted by permission of the publisher; **JOHN CLARE**: 'The Fear of Flowers' and 'The Wheat Ripening' from *Poems [A selection]*, edited by Arthur Symons (Henry Frowde, 1908), reprinted by permission of Brian Read; 'The Maple Tree' from *John Clare: Poems*, edited by Edmund Blunden and Alan Porter (Cobden-Sanderson, 1920); 'The Ragwort' from *Madrigals & Chronicles*, edited by Edmund Blunden (Beaumont Press, 1924); 'March Violet', 'Wood Anemone', 'The Yarrow' and 'The Daisy' from *The Poems of John Clare*, two volumes, edited by J. W. Tibble (J. M. Dent, 1935); **HART CRANE**: 'The Air Plant' and 'Royal Palm' from *Complete Poems of Hart Crane*, edited by Marc Simon (Liveright, 1986), copyright 1933, © 1958, 1966 by Liveright Publishing Corporation, © 1986 by Marc Simon, reprinted by permission of the publisher; **FRED D'AGUIAR**: 'A Gift of a Rose' from *British Subjects* (Bloodaxe Books, 1993), reprinted by permission of the publisher; **RUTH DALLAS**: 'Living with a Cabbage-tree' from *Walking on the Snow* (The Caxton Press, 1976); **EMILY DICKINSON**: #380 ('There Is a Flower That Bees Prefer'), #392 ('Through the Dark Sod'), #440 (''Tis Customary As We Part'), #525 ('I Think the Hemlock Likes to Stand'), #994 ('Partake As Doth The Bee') and #1424 ('The Gentian Has a Parched Corolla') from *The Poems of Emily Dickinson*, edited by Thomas H. Johnson (Cambridge, Mass.: The Belknap Press of Harvard University Press, 1955), © 1951, 1955, 1979 by the President and Fellows of Harvard College, reprinted by permission of the publisher; **PETER DIDSBURY**: 'Roses' from *The Butchers of Hull* (Bloodaxe Books, 1982), reprinted by permission of the publisher; **RITA DOVE**: 'Then Came Flowers' from *Selected Poems* (Vintage, 1993), reprinted by permission of the author; **BASIL DU TOIT**: 'Thorn Trees' from *The Heart in Exile:*

South African Poetry in English, 1990–1995, edited by Leon de Kock and Ian Tromp (Penguin Books, 1996); **LAURIS EDMOND**: 'Jonquils' from *In Position* (Bloodaxe Books, 1997), reprinted by permission of the publisher; **RUTH FAINLIGHT**: 'Autumn Crocus' from *Sugar-Paper Blue* (Bloodaxe Books, 1997), reprinted by permission of the author and publisher; **VICKI FEAVER**: 'Marigolds' and 'White Tulips' from *The Handless Maiden* (Jonathan Cape, 1994), reprinted by permission of The Random House Group Ltd; **ROBERT FROST**: 'Birches' from *The Poetry of Robert Frost*, edited by Edward Connery Lathem (Jonathan Cape, 1969), © 1969 by Henry Holt & Co., reprinted by permission of The Random House Group Ltd on behalf of the Estate of Robert Frost, and Henry Holt & Co., LLC; **ALICE FULTON**: 'Forcing White Lilacs' and 'Rose Fever' from *Dance Script with Electric Ballerina* (University of Illinois Press, 1983), © 1983, 1996 by Alice Fulton, reprinted by permission of the author and publisher; **ALLEN GINSBERG**: 'Sunflower Sutra' from *Selected Poems 1947–1995* (Penguin Books, 1997; first published in *Howl, Before & After: San Francisco Bay Area* (1955–1956)), © Allen Ginsberg, 1996, reprinted by permission of Penguin UK; **LOUISE GLUCK**: 'Ipomoea' , 'Lamium', 'Snowdrops', 'Trillium' and 'The Wild Iris' from *The Wild Iris* (Carcanet Press, 1992), and 'Mock Orange' from *The Triumph of Achilles* (Ecco Press, 1985) in *The First Five Books of Poems* (Carcanet Press, 1997), reprinted by permission of the author and publisher; **LORNA GOODISON**: 'A Bed of Mint' and 'About the Tamarind' from *Guinea Woman* (Carcanet Press, 2000), reprinted by permission of the author and publisher; **JORIE GRAHAM**: 'I Was Taught Three' and 'Opulence' from *The Dream of the Unified Field* (Carcanet Press, 1996), reprinted by permission of the author and publisher; **THOM GUNN**: 'The Cherry Tree' and 'Mandrakes' from *Collected Poems* (Faber & Faber, 1993), reprinted by permission of the publisher; **H.D. (HILDA DOOLITTLE)**: 'Pear Tree' from *Collected Poems 1912–1944* (Carcanet Press, 1984), © 1982 by The Estate of Hilda Doolittle, reprinted by permission of Carcanet Press and New Directions Publishing Corporation; **IAN HAMILTON**: 'Rose' from *Sixty Poems* (Faber & Faber, 1998), reprinted by permission of the publisher; **ROBERT HAYDEN**: 'The Night-Blooming Cereus' from *The Collected Poems of Robert Hayden*, edited by Frederick Glaysher (Liveright, 1972), © 1972 by Robert Hayden, reprinted by permission of Liveright Publishing Corporation; **SEAMUS**

HEANEY: 'Whinlands' from *Door into the Dark* (Faber & Faber, 1969), 'The Haw Lantern' from *The Haw Lantern* (Faber & Faber, 1987), and 'Mint' and 'The Poplar' from *The Spirit Level* (Faber & Faber, 1996), reprinted by permission of the publisher; **SELIMA HILL**: 'My Father's Tulips', reprinted by permission of the author; **A. E. HOUSMAN**: 'It nods and curtseys and recovers' and 'Loveliest of Trees, the Cherry Now' from *The Collected Poems of A. E. Housman* (Henry Holt, 1940), © 1939, 1940, 1965 by Henry Holt & Co, and 1967 by Robert E. Symons, reprinted by permission of The Society of Authors as the Literary Representative of the Estate of A. E. Housman and Henry Holt & Co., LLC; **LANGSTON HUGHES**: 'Magnolia Flowers' from *Selected Poems* (Serpent's Tail, 1999), reprinted by permission of David Higham Associates; **TED HUGHES**: 'Snowdrop' from *Lupercal* (Faber & Faber, 1960), 'Thistles' from *Wodwo* (Faber & Faber, 1967), 'Rhododendrons' and 'Heather' from *Remains of Elmet* (Faber & Faber, 1979), 'Big Poppy', 'Sketch of a Goddess' and 'Sunstruck Foxglove' from *Flowers and Insects* (Faber & Faber, 1986), and 'Daffodils' from *Birthday Letters* (Faber & Faber, 1998), reprinted by permission of the publisher; **ROBIN HYDE**: 'Chrysanthemum' from *Persephone in Winter* (Hurst & Blackett, 1937), reprinted by permission of Derek Challis for the Estate of Robin Hyde; **KATHLEEN JAMIE**: 'Meadowsweet' and 'Rhododendrons' from *Jizzen* (Picador, 1999), reprinted by permission of the author and Macmillan Publishers Ltd; and 'Speirin', published by permission of the author; **JACKIE KAY**: 'Keeping Orchids' from *Other Lovers* (Bloodaxe Books, 1993), reprinted by permission of the publisher; **JANE KENYON**: 'Peonies at Dusk' from *Otherwise: New and Selected Poems* (Graywolf Press, 1996), © 1996 by the Estate of Jane Kenyon, reprinted by permission of Graywolf Press, Saint Paul, Minnesota; **MIMI KHALVATI**: 'Why Does the Aspen Tremble?' from *Selected Poems* (Carcanet Press, 2001), reprinted by permission of the author and publisher; **AUGUST KLEINZAHLER**: 'Peaches in November' from *Red Sauce, Whiskey and Snow* (Faber & Faber, 1995), © 1995 by August Kleinzahler, and 'Poppies in the Wind' from *Live from the Hong Kong Nile Club* (Faber & Faber, 2000), © 2000 by August Kleinzahler, reprinted by permission of Faber & Faber Ltd and Farrar, Straus & Giroux LLC; 'The Gardenia' and 'Hollyhocks in the Fog', reprinted by permission of the author; **STANLEY KUNITZ**: 'Approach of Autumn' from *The Collected Poems* (W. W. Norton, 2000), reprinted by permission of the publisher; **JAMES LASDUN**: 'Oxblood' and 'Timing' from *The Revenant* (Jonathan Cape, 1995), reprinted by permission of the author; **DENISE LEVERTOV**: 'Brother Ivy' from *A Door in the Hive* (Bloodaxe Books, 1993); **PHILIP LEVINE**: 'Milkweed' from *New Selected Poems* (Alfred A. Knopf, 1991), reprinted by permission of the author; **MICHAEL LONGLEY**: 'Poppies' and 'Ghost Orchid' from *The Ghost Orchid* (Jonathan Cape, 1995), 'Self-heal' and 'Gorse Fires' from *Selected Poems* (Jonathan Cape, 1998), and 'Heartsease', 'The Blackthorn' and 'The Daffodils' from *The Weather in Japan* (Jonathan Cape, 2000), reprinted by permission of the author; **MALCOLM LOWRY**: 'The Wild Cherry' from *The Collected Poetry* (University of British Columbia Press, 1992), copyright by Malcolm Lowry Estate, reprinted by permission of Sterling Lord Literistic Inc; **THOMAS LYNCH**: 'Loneliest of Trees, the Winter Oak' from *Still Life in Milford* (Jonathan Cape, 1998), reprinted by permission of the Random House Group Ltd; **NORMAN MACCAIG**: 'Bell Heather' and 'Venus Fly-Trap' from *Collected Poems: New Edition* (Chatto & Windus, 1990), reprinted by permission of The Random House Group Ltd; **HUGH MACDIARMID**: 'The Little White Rose' from *Selected Poetry of Hugh MacDiarmid* (Carcanet Press, 1992), © 1992 by Michael Grieve, reprinted by permission of Carcanet Press Ltd and New Directions Publishing Corporation; **JAY MACPHERSON**: 'Mandrake' from *Poems Twice Told: The Boatman and Welcoming Disaster* (Oxford University Press, 1981), © Oxford University Press Canada, 1981, reprinted by permission of the publisher; **JACK MAPANJE**: 'Seasoned Jacarandas' from *The Chattering Wagtails of Mikuyu Prison* (Heinemann, 1993), reprinted by permission of Heinemann Educational Publishers; 'The Acacias of Gaborone City, Botswana' from *Skipping Without Ropes* (Bloodaxe Books, 1998), reprinted by permission of the publisher; **MEDBH MCGUCKIAN**: from 'The Orchid House' in *The Flower Master and Other Poems* (The Gallery Press, 1993), reprinted by permission of the publisher; **JAMIE MCKENDRICK**: 'The Century Plant' from *Sky Tails* (Faber & Faber, 2000), reprinted by permission of the publisher; 'Chrome Yellow', reprinted by permission of the author; **SANDRA MCPHERSON**: 'Phlox Diffusa' from *Edge Effect: Trails and Portrayals* (Wesleyan University Press, 1996), reprinted by permission of the author and publisher; **W. S. MERWIN**: 'The Palms' from *Travels* (Alfred A. Knopf, 1993), reprinted by permission of David Higham Associates; **CHRISTO-**

PHER MIDDLETON: 'Avocada Plant' from *111 Poems* (Carcanet Press, 1983), reprinted by permission of the author and publisher; **MARIANNE MOORE**: 'Rosemary' and 'The Sycamore' from *Complete Poems* (Faber & Faber, 1968), reprinted by permission of the publisher; **BLAKE MORRISON**: 'Cuckoo-pint' from *Selected Poems* (Granta Books, 1999), reprinted by permission of Peters Fraser & Dunlop Group on behalf of Blake Morrison; **SEITLHAMO MOTSAPI**: 'a roses for the folks we know' from *Earthstepper/The Ocean is Very Shallow* (Deep South Publishers, 1995), reprinted by permission of the author; **LES MURRAY**: 'Lotus Dam' and 'Flowering Eucalypt in Autumn' from *Collected Poems* (Carcanet Press, 1998), reprinted by permission of the author and publisher; '*Angophora Floribunda*', published by permission of the author; **HOWARD NEMEROV**: 'Dandelions' from *The Salt Garden* (Little, Brown & Company, 1955), and 'Ginkgoes in Fall' from *The Collected Poems of Howard Nemerov* (University of Chicago Press, 1977), reprinted by permission of Margaret Nemerov; **NORMAN NICHOLSON**: 'The Burning Rose' from *The Collected Poems* (Faber & Faber, 1994), reprinted by permission of David Higham Associates; **OODGEROO NOONUCCAL**: 'Municipal Gum Tree' from *Inside Black Australia: An Anthology of Aboriginal Poetry* (Penguin Books Australia, 1988), reprinted by permission of the publisher; **SHARON OLDS**: 'My Mother's Pansies' from *Blood, Tin, Straw* (Jonathan Cape, 2000), reprinted by permission of the Random House Group Ltd; **MARY OLIVER**: 'Moccasin Flowers' from *New and Selected Poems* (Beacon Press, 1992); **ERIC ORMSBY**: 'Live Oak, with Bromeliads' and 'Skunk Cabbage' from *Coastlines* (ECW Press, 1992), © ECW Press, reprinted by permission of ECW Press, Toronto and Montreal; **CHRIS ORSMAN**: 'Ornamental Gorse' from *Ornamental Gorse* (Victoria University Press, 1994); **RUTH PADEL**: 'Rosa Silvestris Russica' from *Angel* (Bloodaxe Books, 1993), reprinted by permission of the author; **DOROTHY PARKER**: 'One Perfect Rose' from *Collected Dorothy Parker* (Penguin Twentieth-Century Classics, 1989), reprinted by permission of Gerald Duckworth & Co Ltd; **DON PATERSON**: 'Twinflooer', published by permission of the author; **TOM PAULIN**: from 'The Book of Juniper' in *Liberty Tree* (Faber & Faber, 1983), and 'Sparrowgrass' from *Walking a Line* (Faber & Faber, 1994), reprinted by permission of the publisher; **RUTH PITTER**: 'Morning Glory', 'The Cedar', 'The Strawberry Plant' and 'The

Tuft of Violets' from *Collected Poems* (Enitharmon Press, 1996), reprinted by permission of the publisher; **SYLVIA PLATH**: 'Among the Narcissi', 'Poppies in July', 'Poppies in October' and 'Tulips' from *Collected Poems*, edited by Ted Hughes (Faber & Faber, 1981), reprinted by permission of the publisher; **EZRA POUND**: 'Alba' from *Collected Shorter Poems* (Faber & Faber, 1968), © 1926 by Ezra Pound, reprinted by permission of Faber & Faber Ltd and New Directions Publishing Corporation; **DUDLEY RANDALL**: 'Roses and Revolutions' from *Poem Counterpoem, Cities Burning* (Broadside Press, 1969), © 1966 by Margaret Danner and Dudley Randall; **PETER REDGROVE**: 'Of Prick-bush' from *The First Earthquake* (Secker & Warburg, 1989), reprinted by permission of the Random House Group Ltd; **LIZETTE WOODWORTH REESE**: 'A Flower of Mullein' from *The Selected Poems of Lizette Woodworth Reese* (Harcourt Rinehart & Winston, 1926); **JAMES REISS**: 'Lily' from *Ten Thousand Good Mornings* (Carnegie Mellon University Press, 2001), reprinted by permission of the author; **ADRIENNE RICH**: 'The Corpse-Plant' and 'The Knot' from *Collected Early Poems: 1950–1970* (W. W. Norton, 1993), reprinted by permission of the author and publisher; **ANNE RIDLER**: 'Snakeshead Fritillaries' from *Collected Poems* (Carcanet Press, 1994), reprinted by permission of the author and publisher; **ROBIN ROBERTSON**: 'Making the Green One Red', published by permission of the author; **ROLAND ROBINSON**: 'Casuarina' from *Selected Poems* (Angus & Robertson, 1983), reprinted by permission of HarperCollins Publishers Australia; **THEODORE ROETHKE**: 'Carnations', © 1946 by Editorial Publications Inc, 'Orchids', © 1948 by Theodore Roethke, and 'The Geranium, © 1963 by Beatrice Roethke, administratrix of the Estate of Theodore Roethke,' from *Collected Poems* (Faber & Faber, 1968), reprinted by permission of Faber & Faber Ltd, and Doubleday, a division of Random House Inc; **MURIEL RUKEYSER**: 'Fighting for Roses' from *The Collected Poems of Muriel Rukeyser* (McGraw-Hill, 1978), reprinted by permission of International Creative Management Inc; **JAMES SCHUYLER**: 'The Bluet' from *Collected Poems* (Farrar, Straus & Giroux, 1993), © 1993 by the Estate of James Schuyler, reprinted by permission of the publisher; **E. J. SCOVELL**: 'Deaths of Flowers' from *Collected Poems* (Carcanet, 1988), © E. J. Scovell, 1988, reprinted by permission of Cathy Buffonge and the publisher; **SENI SENEVIRATNE**: 'Cinnamon Roots', reprinted by permission of the author; **OLIVE SENIOR**:

'Starapple' from *Gardening in the Tropics* (Bloodaxe Books, 1995), reprinted by permission of McClelland & Stewart Inc; **VIKRAM SETH**: 'Evening Wheat' from *The Humble Administrator's Garden* (Carcanet Press, 1985), © Vikram Seth, 1985, reprinted by permission of Curtis Brown Ltd (Edinburgh); **ANNE SEXTON**: 'Red Roses' from *The Complete Poems of Anne Sexton* (Houghton Mifflin, 1981), © Anne Sexton, reprinted by permission of Sterling Lord Literistic Inc; **ANNE STEVENSON**: 'Himalayan Balsam' from *The Collected Poems 1955–1995* (Bloodaxe Books, 2000) reprinted by permission of the publisher; **MYRNA STONE**: 'Wild Onion' from *Poetry* (February 2001), © Modern Poetry Association, reprinted by permission of the author and publisher; **MATTHEW SWEENEY**: 'Cacti' from *Cacti* (Secker & Warburg, 1992), reprinted by permission of the author; **MAY SWENSON**: 'Little Lion Face' from *In Other Words: New Poems* (Alfred A. Knopf, 1987), reprinted by permission of the Literary Estate of May Swenson; **JANET SYLVESTER**: 'Goatsbeard' from *The Mark of Flesh* (W. W. Norton, 1997), © 1997 by Janet Sylvester, reprinted by permission of the publisher; **R. S. THOMAS**: 'Cyclamen' from *Collected Poems 1945–1990* (J. M. Dent, 1993), reprinted by permission of Orion Publishing Group; **FRED VOSS**: 'A Threat' from *Carnegie Hall with Tin Walls* (Bloodaxe Books, 1998), reprinted by permission of the publisher; **DEREK WALCOTT**: 'The Almond Trees' from *The Castaway and Other Poems* (Jonathan Cape, 1965), and 'The Harvest' from *Poems 1965–1980* (Jonathan Cape, 1992), reprinted by permission of The Random House Group Ltd; **TED WALKER**: 'Cuckoo-Pint' from *Fox on a Barn Door: Poems 1963–4* (Jonathan Cape, 1965), reprinted by permission of The Random House Group Ltd; **CHRIS WALLACE-CRABBE**: 'Jasmine' from *Selected Poems 1956–1994* (Oxford University Press, 1995), reprinted by permission of Carcanet Press Ltd; **RICHARD WILBUR**: 'Thyme Flowering Among Rocks' from *New and Collected Poems* (Faber & Faber, 1988), reprinted by permission of the author; **C. K. WILLIAMS**: 'Elms' from *New and Selected Poems* (Bloodaxe Books, 1995), reprinted by permission of the publisher; **WILLIAM CARLOS WILLIAMS**: 'Queen-Ann's-Lace' and 'Young Sycamore' from *Collected Poems of William Carlos Williams, 1909–1939, Volume 1* (Carcanet Press, 1987), © 1938 by New Directions Publishing Corporation, reprinted by permission of New Directions Publishing Corporation and Carcanet Press Ltd; **JAMES WRIGHT**: 'To the Saguaro Cactus Tree in the

Desert Rain' from *Above the River: The Complete Poems* (Bloodaxe Books, 1992), reprinted by permission of Sheil Land Associates Ltd; **JUDITH WRIGHT**: 'Words, Roses, Stars' from *Collected Poems 1942–1985* (Carcanet Press, 1994), reprinted by permission of HarperCollins Publishers Australia; 'Flame-Tree in a Quarry', 'Phaius Orchid', 'The Hawthorn Hedge' and 'The Cyrads' from *Collected Poems 1942–1985* (Carcanet Press, 1994); **W. B. YEATS**: 'The Rose Tree' and 'The Rose of the World' from *Collected Poems* (Macmillan, 1950), reprinted by permission of A. P. Watt Ltd on behalf of Michael B. Yeats.

Every effort has been made to trace or contact all copyright holders. Chatto & Windus would be pleased to rectify any omissions brought to their notice at the earliest opportunity.

Index of Poets

Walker, Ted, 1934–, England 24
Wallace-Crabbe, Chris, 1934–, Australia 185
Waller, Edmund, 1606–87, England 264
Whitman, Walt, 1819–92, United States 112
Wilbur, Richard, 1921–, United States 137–8
Wilkinson, Iris Guiver *see* 'Hyde, Robin'
Williams, C. K., 1936–, United States 306
Williams, William Carlos, 1883–1963, United States 3, 307
Wither, George, 1588–1667, England 65–6
Woodworth Reese, Lizette, 1856–1935, United States 293
Wordsworth, William, 1770–1850, England 19, 232
Wright, James, 1927–80, United States 44
Wright, Judith, 1915–2000, Australia 91, 199, 233–4, 249, 297
Yeats, W. B., 1865–1939, Ireland 250, 254

Index of Titles

Index of First Lines